Spreading
the Word

Spreading the Word

Language and Dialect in America

JOHN McWHORTER

HEINEMANN
Portsmouth, NH

Heinemann
A division of Reed Elsevier Inc.
361 Hanover Street
Portsmouth, NH 03801–3912
www.heinemann.com

Offices and agents throughout the world

Library of Congress Cataloging-in-Publication Data
McWhorter, John H.
    Spreading the word : language and dialect in America / John McWhorter.
      p.   cm.
    Includes bibliographical references and index.
    ISBN 0-325-00198-7
    1. United States—Languages—Variation.   2. English language—Variation—United States.
3. Language and languages—Variation.   4. Languages, Mixed.   I. Title.
P381.U54M38   2000
427'.973—dc21   99-42846
                                                         CIP

Editor: Lois Bridges
Production: Abigail M. Heim
Cover design: Joni Doherty Design
Cover photograph: Joel Brown
Manufacturing: Deanna Richardson

Printed in the United States of America on acid-free paper
03   02   DA   3   4   5

Contents

Acknowledgments

Thanks to Ashlee Bailey for taking the time to read each chapter as it rolled out of the printer and give useful editorial and conceptual comments; to Jonathan Barnes, Stéphane Goyette, Rich Rhodes, and Christy Wills for language data; Belén Flores, Orin Gensler, Kevin Moore, and Maria Troniak for keeping my own language data honest; and to my editor Lois Bridges for support far beyond the call of duty.

Introduction

Growing up in America, it is impossible to avoid being inculcated with a particular conception of what "English" is. This conception is so deeply ingrained that we rarely have a sense of it being "taught" at all. I refer to the basic idea that the English of *Good Morning America* and *Newsweek* is the "good," "default," "best" English, whereas other dialects, such as Joe Pesci's Brooklynese, rappers' Black English, and Jeff Foxworthy's Southern "redneck" dialect, are violations of, or lapses from, "good" English.

Our opinions of these dialects vary according to the contexts they are used in, our personal background, and the place of their speakers in society. Yet whether we find these dialects debased or cute, there is always a fundamental sense that they are evidence of grungy mitts leaving their prints on the cool, clean formica of standard English, and that in a perfect world, everyone would Straighten Up and Talk Right, just as they would pay all their taxes, be strict serial monogamists, and floss every night.

The idea that there is one "best" English shining in the sky is so intuitively plausible, and so relentlessly hammered into us throughout our lives, that it is natural for teachers to consider part of their jobs to be upholding standard English. Of course, in a way it is—a mastery of spoken and written standard English is necessary for almost any kind of success in our society. However, we are misled in thinking of varieties of English other than the standard as "wrong": as it happens, this idea is as erroneous as similarly attractive ones such as that the earth is flat. We will see in this book that other kinds of English are not bastardizations of standard English but variations upon the basic plan of English, of which the standard is but one.

Of course, we could go through life thinking the earth is flat and suffer no ill consequences. However, understanding the truth about English is particularly important for teachers because it changes our perspective on how to impart standard English to our students. Specifically, rather than approach other kinds of English as something to teach students out of, we can celebrate the other kinds of English they speak, as well as other kinds, while *adding* standard English as a new part of their repertoires.

As we become accustomed to seeing our students' dialect repertoires not as a collection of bad habits but as a kind of smorgasbord, in time teachers in America will also find themselves adjusting to an even more striking kind of diversity. Increasingly, teachers all over America are finding that not just the occasional student, but often *most* of their students, speak languages other than English at home. As I write, almost 10 percent of the United States population is foreign born, and whites have become a numerical minority in the California. The languages most often encountered today, such as Chinese, Russian, and Tagalog, are different from English in ways many of us would never even think was possible in a language.

This, too, is a possible source of enrichment for classroom teaching, giving a precious opportunity for schoolchildren to become acquainted with the richness of foreign languages with living demonstrations—each other—rather than having such things simply laid out on a blackboard. Thus, in this book we will also get a quick tour through eight of the languages that more and more American schoolchildren are dreaming in every day.

Spreading
the Word

1

—

"I Hear So Much Bad Grammar These Days"

The most important thing to internalize in order to understand the truth about English is something that may at first seem somewhat irrelevant to the issue. Namely, all languages are always in the process of gradually changing into new ones.

Like evolution, this process is a slow one, barely perceptible within a human lifetime. The only aspect of it we perceive consciously is the constant turnover of slang. For example, as I write this, the expression *She's all that* is being used to describe a woman who is sexually attractive and perhaps also knows it in a stylishly self-assured way; the popularity of the expression has just been enshrined in a movie title. In the early 1990s, the expression *She's got it going on* was used to connote roughly the same thing; for a while in the 1980s she was *fresh,* in the 1970s she was a *freak,* in the 1950s a *hot tomato,* in the 1920s she *had that thing,* and so on.

This, however, is only the very surface of what I mean by the fact that language is always changing. Slang expressions, like fashion trends, come and go by the decade (or half decade) as the underlying "neutral" language sits and watches—for example, while *She's got that thing* is now opaque and *She's all that* will probably sound rather *ten minutes ago* by the time this book is published, *She's beautiful* would be comprehensible to a 90-year-old who once said *She's got that thing* as well as to the teenager today impressed by the *all that* in question.

Yet even the neutral language only sits and watches for so long: in other words, even the very basic "vanilla" part of language is always in a state of gradual change. What this means is that there is no society on earth where people could manage a conversation with their ancestors from a thousand years back or more.

Language on the Move

Here, for example, is what the English Lord's Prayer looked like in 1000 A.D.:

Fæder ūre, thū the eart on heofonum, sī thīn nama gehālgod.
Father our you that are in heaven be your name blessed

Ūrne gedæghwāmlīcan hlāf syle ūs tō dæg
our daily bread give us today

This is the direct ancestor to the English I am writing in, and yet to us it is nothing less than a foreign tongue. We must remember that this is not some funny way certain people promenading around drafty castles in heavy clothes talked—this was the way all English looked.

As we said, however, language is always changing. As such, here is the same passage in English as it was three hundred years later:

Fader oure that is i heuen, blessid be thi name.
Oure ilk day bred gif us to day.

Here we don't even need the word-by-word translation (except for *ilk,* which means "each," and thus "each-day bread" instead of "daily bread"), but it is still quite unlike any English we would encounter anywhere today, and would be only partly comprehensible to us as spoken. The transition from one stage to another was gradual, barely perceptible to most people within their lifetimes. Yet centuries of gradual changes took English speakers from that prickly-looking Germanic tongue we barely recognize to the language of Ted Koppel (another prickly looking Germanic, but still).

How is it that we get from something like *fæder ūre* to *our father?* First of all, the meaning of even basic words is always gradually changing in a language. For example, in Old English, the word *bread* referred to all food, and what we call bread was *hlāf.* Gradually, *bread* came to have the more specialized Wonder-ful meaning we know, and *hlāf,* gradually pronounced *loaf,* moved over and became even more specialized, referring to one form bread can take. This kind of thing is not an occasional case, but the default case, and is often even more extreme—*nice* used to mean "silly," and the word *silly* itself originally meant "blessed"!

In addition, the basic sounds of a language are constantly wearing down, with new ones being created. *Dæg* for "day" in Old English has long lost the final *g,* and *nama* for "name" has long lost the final *a,* although the spelling reflects the stage when it was halfway along the way to disappearing, when the sound was like the *a* in *about*. At the same time, however, new sounds were developing: the first *a* in *nama*, which was pronounced like the *a* in *father*, became two sounds *ay* and *ee*, such that today we say *nay-eem*. Old English didn't even have *v* at first—it's no accident that *heavens* is *heofonum*—the sound developed over time in English.

Similarly, endings are constantly shorn off and re-created. Notice that "our" in the Old English is *ūre* with "father" but *ūrne* with "daily bread." The difference is because Old English speakers used different forms depending on how a noun was used in the sentence: because *daily bread* is an object (*give us our daily bread*), the word for *our* had to take a certain ending. In the same way, the *-um* of *heofonum* "heaven" was required because the word was used with a preposition. Almost all of these endings were gradually lost as English changed, with our possessive *'s* being the only ending now regularly used. Conversely, though, new endings develop. The *-ly* in *sweetly* began as the separate word *like*, and gradually became a part of the word it came after. Almost all endings begin as separate words in this way.

Even basic word order changes: today anyone who said "the bread please pass" would not date much, but it was par for the course in Old English. Today, occasional frozen phrases like "darling mine" feel archaic, because they are—in Old English "father our" was quite normal.

The next thing that is important about how language changes is that any change can take place in various directions, just like the shrew-like creatures who were the first mammals evolved here into elephants, there into cats, here into monkeys, and there into whales. For example, as the Roman Empire broke up, Latin evolved into the various Romance languages, such as French, Spanish, Italian, Portuguese, and Romanian. Each language was the result of Latin undergoing thousands of changes, none of which anyone could have predicted at the time.

The Latin word for *have*, for example, was *habēre*. In French this word became *avoir*—ah-VWAR—and in Spanish *haber*—ah-BEAR. In both cases, the final *e* of *habēre* dropped off like the final *a* of Old English *nama* did, and the initial *h* did as well, just as the *g* dropped off the end of *dæg*. However, as Latin changed into French, the *b* in *habēre* became a *v* just as the *f* in Old English *heofonum* became a *v*. But in Spanish it happened to stay *b* just as the *d* in *dæg* stayed *d*. On the other hand, Spanish kept the first *e* in *habēre* while French turned it into the "wa" sound of *oi*. Finally, Spanish doesn't even use *haber* to mean "to have" in the basic sense anymore. *Haber* is used in constructions like "I had spoken" *yo había hablado,* but the literal word for "have" is *tener*, whose ancestor in Latin had meant "to hold" (and whose French version *tenir* still does). Thus, in Spanish, the Latin word for "hold", a specific kind of having, evolved into meaning a more general kind of having, just as in English *bird* used to mean only little tweeters like sparrows and *fowl* was the general word for things with feathers, but now *fowl* is a marginal word and *bird* means any bird. To an Anglo-Saxon we would look funny calling an eagle a "bird," and to an Ancient Roman, Spaniards would look funny talking about "holding" an apartment by the sea.

As the result of changes like this transforming Latin in several separate places, the Latin sentence "I gave it to the woman":

> Feminae id dedi
> woman-to it gave-I

was gradually transformed in France, Spain, Italy, Portugal, and Romania into sentences that a Roman would barely recognize as having anything to do with their speech, even on paper:

French:	Je l'ai donné à la femme.
Spanish:	Se lo dí a la mujer.
Italian:	L'ho datto alla donna.
Portuguese:	O dei à mulher.
Romanian:	Am dat-o femeii.

This kind of transformation has produced every language on earth. English developed from a lost Germanic ancestor, which also developed into German, Dutch, Swedish, Icelandic, and others; Arabic, Hebrew, and the Amharic that Ethiopians speak developed from a Semitic ancestor; Hawaiian, Maori in New Zealand, and the Tahitian that Cézanne heard all developed from a single original Polynesian ancestor.

How Dialects Arise

What does all this have to do with dialects in America? This: dialects of a language are all the result of the exact same kind of gradual change as different languages are; the difference is simply that in dialects, the change has not gone far enough to produce what we would process as different languages. Here are some British English dialect samples:

Lancashire:	Ween meet neaw ta'en a hawse steyler at wur mayin' off with'tit.
	"We have just now taken a horse stealer who was making off with it."
Cornwall:	Aw bain't gwine for tell ee.
	"He isn't going to tell you."

Scots:	Efter he had gane throu the haill o it, a fell faimin brak out i yon laund.
	"After he had gone through all of it, a great famine broke out in the land."
Nottinghamshire:	Tha mun come one naight ter th' cottage, afore tha goos; sholl ter?
	"You must come one night to the cottage before you go, will you?"

As odd as these passages appear to us, we process all of them as falling under the banner of "English" in the same way as ostriches are birds to us even though they don't fly and penguins are too even though they swim and wear suits. Clearly, these aren't what we call separate languages in the sense that French is a different language from Spanish. Yet all of these varieties evolved through the exact same types of processes that turned Latin into the Romance languages or that turned Sanskrit into Hindi, Gujarati, and Bengali—it's just that the process hasn't proceeded as far.

The people who turned Latin into French obviously had no contact with the ones on the other side of Europe turning it into Romanian, and thus the changes went on their merry independent ways and eventually resulted in "Latins" that were mutually unintelligible—that is, separate languages. On the other hand, the people developing these English dialects, all sharing the little island of Britain, had contact with one another, as well as with the standard variety of English. Thus, they ended up making the same or similar changes as often as making quirky individual ones, and stayed akin in a way that the Romance languages did not need to.

Once again, this is typical—most languages exist in an array of dialects that differ the way these British ones do, and often more. The standard variety of a language is but one of many flavors it comes in. For example, here is a sentence of standard French contrasted with the colloquial Canadian French equivalent that Jack Kerouac, child of French Canadians, grew up hearing:

Parisian French:	Où étais-tu, toi? Ça te tente de venir maintenant?
Canadian French:	Où c'est que t'étais, twe? Ça te tente-tu de venir à cette heure?
	"Where were you? Do you feel like coming now?"

One does not even have to know French to see the differences here, and they are simply due to changes having proceeded differently in Canada than in

France, just as changes in Latin proceeded differently in France than they did in Spain. Italian comes in an even wider range of flavors. If we take Italian in school, we learn to say *Chi hai visto?* for "Who did you see?" but in the Romagnolo dialect, the sentence is *Chi che t'è vest?* This kind of variation is why Italian-Americans' Sicilian grandparents say *manigawt* for what we see written on the container as *manicotti* in standard Italian. It's the same everywhere—German, Arabic, Finnish, Japanese, Spanish, Serbo-Croatian, you name it. Viewed close up, a language is a bundle of dialects. To be presented with only, say, standard German as "German" is analogous to being presented with a picture of a beagle as a "dog"—just as the beagle is only one of hundreds of variations on the "dog" theme, standard German is but one of myriad "Germans"; someone from the north of Germany can go to a student pub in the South of Germany and barely make out what people are saying.

We are now in a position to get down to cases and look at dialects in America through a new lens. There are six simple points to keep in mind.

1.   *Any dialect you hear, no matter who is speaking it or what they happen to be saying, is the product of the same kind of change that turned Latin into French.* It is very tempting to think that the speech of Rocky Balboa or of young black inner-city teens is somehow a breach of grammar, a deformation of English. Yet these dialects are nothing but products of the same kind of gradual language change that elsewhere turned Latin into French. Just as we do not think of French as a deformation of Latin, a colloquial English dialect is not a deformation of English. We can ask ourselves: if the change from Latin *feminae id dedi* to French *je l'ai donné à la femme* was not a breach of Latin grammar, then how could the progression from *There's nobody here* to *Ain't nobody here* be a breach of English grammar? If the difference between the characters in *The Godfather*'s grandparents' Sicilian and standard Italian is quaint or, for most of us, of no comment, then why is it bad grammar if the characters themselves say *youse guys* instead of *you guys*?

　　The social associations here make it hard for us to see it this way, but the fact is that *youse guys* and *je l'ai donné à la femme* are products of the exact same process. To put a point on it, even *youse guys* and *you guys* are products of the exact same process: in Middle English, *you* was only used to refer to two or more people, while one addressed one person as *thou*. For a long time, using *you* to refer to one person was seen as a barefooted, uncultivated sort of thing, but because language always changes, after a while everybody was using *you* this way, and today we don't even know that it could ever have been any different. But because language always changes, *you* is *still* evolving. Now we

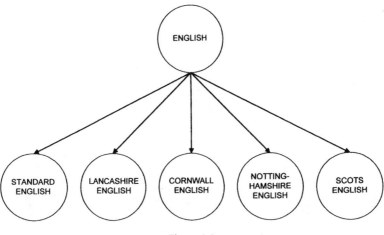

Figure 1.1.

scoff at *youse* as people scoffed at referring to one person as *you* six hundred years ago.

In other words, the colloquial dialects we hear around us are variations upon English, not degradations of it. What we are hearing are today's results of a process ongoing all over the world at all times—language change. Figure 1.1 illustrates development of standard English and dialects. There is something in Figure 1.1 that we might not notice at first, but that is important. It is quite natural for us to think that the colloquial dialects we hear developed *from* standard English. Notice, however, that I have not drawn the colloquial dialects developing from standard English, but alongside them. Thus, our next point.

2.   *Colloquial dialects develop alongside standard varieties, not from them.* The elite associations of standard English are such that even if we accept that language change is transformation rather than decay, if we think that the colloquial dialects evolved from the standard, then it is tricky to shake associating these dialects with decline: it is difficult to sense the development from *Masterpiece Theatre* to *The Dukes of Hazzard* as a straight line rather than a fall. In this light, it helps us to remember that colloquial English dialects are not only products of the same *type* of change as standard English, but of the same *source* of change as standard English: Old English. In other words, it is natural to think that Figure 1.2 shows what happened when in fact Figure 1.1 is more accurate. This makes it even clearer how equal all of these varieties are in "God's eyes": the English of the "hillbilly" chasing Bugs Bunny is equal

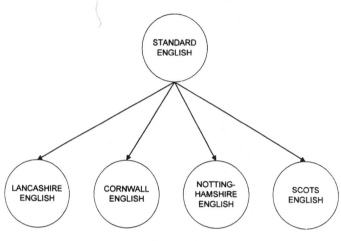

Figure 1.2.

to the English of the characters on *Friends,* just as Spanish is equal to French, just as a schnauzer is equal to a golden retriever, just as a tetra is to a goldfish.

Yet some of us might ask, "Even if the standard and the other dialects developed alongside each other, doesn't the fact that one of them is standard mean that it was somehow the better one?" This intelligent question leads us to the next important point.

3. *Standard dialects are chosen according to geopolitical accident, not according to anything inherent to the dialect itself.* For example, English comes in many varieties in Great Britain, many of them almost stretching our sense of what English even is. Yet the reason the dialect we know as the standard became coin of the realm was not because it was more logical or better sounding than the others. It just happened that this dialect was the one that had evolved in the region where London was. When London became the center of commerce and culture, with the great universities of Oxford and Cambridge arising in the area as a result, the dialect that happened to have evolved there, spoken by educated and powerful people, was gradually chosen as the one used in writing, as the one taught, and inevitably as a result, came to be viewed as the "best" dialect.

This choice was as arbitrary as the fact that in the early 1980s, the torn sweatshirt that Jennifer Beals wore in the movie *Flashdance* became a fashion craze because Beals was lovely, the movie was a hit, and its soundtrack was coming out of our bathroom faucets for a year. If you think about it, what's so great about a torn sweatshirt? If Roseanne Barr had worn one for a whole season of *Roseanne,* not a single woman in America would have taken out scissors to rip up her nice sweatshirts; what made this make sense in 1983 was a random confluence of glamour and sensory overload. It was the same with the East Midlands dialect that became standard English.

"French" was a squishy concept in the area now known as France, comprising a range of varieties many not even mutually intelligible. In the north and west were the varieties that were imported to Canada to become today's Canadian French, which takes someone schooled in Parisian French weeks to catch on to. In the south, travelling musicians were writing love songs in Provençal, so different from Parisian French that it is today considered a separate language Occitan, which even French speakers have to learn as a separate tongue. When Paris became the center of power, the variety of French spoken there was established as the standard, with the other varieties quite deliberately recast as dialects not to be taught in school, not even the vastly different Occitan. All of this is due to mere politics and chance. There was nothing about Parisian French that made it inherently somehow "the one". After all, what remains some of the world's most sublime music had been written in the Provençal, which is now considered the subliterate "patois" of rural folk, simply because it was not where the geopolitical action happened to settle.

What this means is that quite literally, if we could roll the historical dice again and the capital of England had become Edinburgh, then the "right" English would be much like the Scottish example on page 5, and the dialect we know as standard would be as quaint to our ears as the Nottinghamshire dialect, which is spoken by the gardener boytoy in *Lady Chatterley's Lover*.

Here in America, we have seen firsthand how arbitrary the choice of a standard is. From the beginning of American history until the middle of the twentieth century, the "best" English was considered to be that spoken by moneyed people in large northeastern cities, which had a distinctly English air to the modern ear. Old movie stars often learned this dialect if they didn't already speak it, which is why Bette Davis at the end of *Now, Voyager* says "Why reach for the moon when we have the stahs?" There is an old newsreel of Franklin D. Roosevelt's patrician mother giving a salutation to the public, and if you didn't know better you would swear she had been born in London — she sounds so Merchant-Ivory. After World War II, with the country in a drum-banging, red meat mood as the new king of the world, this dialect came to be seen as a tad lavender, and broadcasters gradually opted for a Midwestern dialect as the standard, one often described as "flat" but that had less of the air of tea and crumpets about it, better suiting the new America. Today you can see the transition in the 1950s sitcom *Father Knows Best*, with Robert Young speaking in the Walter Cronkite voice we now think of as "default American" while Jane Wyatt as his wife tells their daughter "You'll have to talk to yaw fah-thuh." Wyatt was born in New Jersey — but to an investment banker of tony heritage with a drama critic wife; this was the way a privileged young girl was taught to speak in the teens and twenties when she grew up. Why is Walter Cronkite's speech somehow more "default English" than Jane Wyatt's, especially when speech similar to hers is still considered "the way" in England? It's all a matter of random accident.

But we still might ask: "Isn't standard English just more complex and subtler than the colloquial dialects?" The answer follows in our next point.

4. *Colloquial dialects are as complex and nuanced as standard ones.* The complexities and shadings of local dialects are not appreciated because they are not studied in schools the way standard dialects are. In addition, the tendency to see colloquial speech as a departure from, rather than an alternative to, the standard variety distracts us from seeing its complexities.

Once again, understanding this at home begins with looking at similar situations far away where sociological factors do not cloud our perceptions. In Bulgarian, the definite article (*the*) comes after the noun rather than coming before it. Thus, "child" is *dete* and "the child" is *dete* **to**. This is how it is in the standard dialect. However, in the rural Trân dialect, there are three kinds of definite article in addition to the *-to* one: one means "the one here"—for example, *dete* **vo** means "the child in front of me." The other means "the child there"—*dete* **no** means "the child over on the other side of the room." In addition, these are only the forms for one class of noun (just like the *-a* of *habla* in Spanish is only appropriate in the present tense for one of three classes of verb). There are two other noun classes with their own forms, plus one plural class with different forms—in other words, there is a special *the* used when a person says "the children over there." This is obviously a more complicated and fine-grained way of handling *the*-ness than anything people who grow up with standard Bulgarian are accustomed to, and certainly unlike our simple little *the*. And yet the people who use this baroque little grid of *the*'s day in and day out are humble, uncultivated folk who would be seen very much as hicks by urban educated Bulgarians.

Along these same lines but right under our noses, Black English provides a good example in its notorious use, or non-use, of the verb *to be*. The general consensus about this is that many black people either drop the verb *to be* or use it all over the place without conjugating it—*I be a student* is the example one hears most often. However, it is not nearly this simple.

Indeed, black speakers often do not use *to be* before nouns and adjectives—*She my sister, He skinny.* As we will see in the next chapter, while this is indeed simpler than standard English, it is not an indication of "primitivity"; it is in fact quite proper in many highly prestigious languages. However, in any case, where *be* is used before verbs, things are actually more complex than standard English.

In standard English, although we are often taught that *I walk* is "present tense", in fact, if someone asked us what we were doing we would never answer *I walk*—we would answer *I am walking. I walk,* if you think about it, describes walking on a regular basis—*I walk on that path whenever there are mushrooms after a rain.*

In Black English, however, there is an explicit marker that something is done on a regular basis. That marker is *be.* Thus, if you asked a Black English speaker what someone was doing, contrary to popular belief, they would never answer *He be walking.* This would sound strange and immediately mark someone as not having grown up speaking the dialect natively. *He be walking* would mean that the person walks every day: *When I be walkin' by his house he always be shoutin' out my name.* The answer to "What is he doing now?" would be *He walkin'.*

Now what our eye goes to first here is that there is no *to be* in *He walkin'*, but actually, in broader view what this means is that Black English has two things to learn—*in'* for right now and *be* for regularly—where standard English only has one, using *-ing* for right now and nothing (*I walk*) for regularly. To a Martian who encountered both dialects and had no idea of the social associations of either one of them, Black English would seem more complex in this regard.

The Martian would also have to learn a special rule for how to form the negative version of one of these sentences. Most of us probably intuit that the negative version of *He walkin'* is *He ain't walkin'.* What, however, is the negative version of *He be walkin'*? *He ain't be walkin'*? You might be able to wrap your head around the notion of a black person saying this, but actually it is as wrong as *Yo hablamos Español*—it has to be *He don't be walkin'.*

So the way black Americans use *be* is not simply a matter of not conjugating *to be* where standard English speakers would. Black English uses this unconjugated *be* in a specific context with a specific meaning—in other words, the black American unconjugated *be* is, of all things, a piece of grammar. If you are not a Black English speaker, next time you are standing in line and people are using the dialect within your earshot, listen for how *be* is used. It will always be in reference to a regular occurrence. In addition, not only will you not hear *I ain't be seein' her no more,* but you will listen in vain for sentences like *I be a court clerk downtown*—*be* is not used with nouns in this way at all. If you are a Black English speaker, think about how you have heard *be* used and you will see that it is a marker of regular activities, not simply an equivalent of *to be* as it is used in standard English—notice how imagining a relative saying *I be her aunt* doesn't sound quite right.

What we are seeing over and over again, then, can be summed up in a fifth basic point.

5. *Our natural sense that one dialect is "better" is based purely on sociological associations, not anything about the dialect itself.* Looking out to sea, it is almost impossible to believe that we are walking around on a sphere rather than on a flat plain. In the same way, it is hard to believe that the "redneck" dialect we associate with rusted old cars in the front yard, the Black English we associate with baggy pants and the inner city, or the Brooklyn English of Marisa Tomei's character in *My Cousin Vinny* could have been enshrined as standard English if the cards had fallen in some other way. It is a little easier to understand this if we take a broader view by taking a look at standard English through the eyes of some outsiders.

For example, in terms of simple aesthetic appeal, standard American English is processed as rather ugly by many Europeans. They flock to it for its usefulness and cachet, of course, but never will you hear a European, or anyone else, talk about how beautiful English is. Compared to the open vowels, crisp, simple, no-nonsense consonants, and musical intonation of Italian, for example, standard English often comes off as a pasty monotone. I remember one German I knew imitating Americans by sneering "white sausage, white sausage" in a nasal voice reminiscent of Mr. Burns' assistant Smithers on *The Simpsons,* and the sad thing is that he *did* sound like an American. On the other hand, Europeans often find Black English rather pretty, and with its more musical intonation reminiscent of that in African languages—think of *Mmmmm-hm!,* black women's wonderful way of saying "You know what *that's* about"—and who's to say they're wrong? Germans in the past were given to worshipping their standard language almost religiously, one philosopher even declaring that the Bible was originally written in it. Yet to many of us, its clusters of consonants make it sound harsh (this is a language where *sexual* is *geschlechtlich:* guh-SHLEKHT-likh, with the *kh* being the gnashing sound of *ch* in *Bach*). To the American ear, the nasal sounds and shifting tones of Chinese sound bizarre—and yet Chinese opera singing is considered heavenly by Chinese people. All of this is simply to show that our judgements on this score are purely arbitrary.

For a long time, the Romance languages were solely spoken varieties while Latin was used in writing. The Berlitz behemoths we now think of as languages were thought of as dialects of Latin and bad ones at that, evidence of the linguistic slovenliness of "the folk." Here is a sniffy comment from this period:

> Spoken Latin has picked up a passel of words considered too casual for
> written Latin, and the grammar people use when speaking has broken

down. The masses barely use anything but the nominative and the accusative . . . it's gotten to the point that the student of Latin is writing in what is to them an artificial language, and it is an effort for him to recite in it decently.

Only when the areas where these "dialects" were spoken coalesced into centralized nations did they come to be thought of as "languages" and written down. French, for example, was first written in a final concession to the fact that Latin was too foreign a language to the general populace to even pretend that they spoke a "dialect" of it anymore. Yet the popular speech that year, 842, was the same as that in 841. What was a lazy "dialect" yesterday was a "language" today, solely because of its sociopolitical associations, not the speech itself. To us, there is nothing "crummy" about this 842 passage of "the Latin of the masses"—it simply looks like something midway along on the path between Latin and French:

The Strasbourg Oaths, 842:

Pro Deo amur et pro christian poblo . . . in quant Deus savir et podir me dunat . . .

Modern French:

Pour l'amour de Dieu et pour le peuple chrétien . . . dans la mesure où Dieu me donne savoir et pouvoir . . .

For the love of God and for the Christian people . . . insofar as God grants me the knowledge and the power . . .

Yet to a Latin-speaking educated cleric this looked like the kind of thing Jeff Foxworthy would do a stand-up routine about in our world.

Another example of how closely tied our judgements of a dialect are to who speaks it is the speech of young "coloured" people in the Cape Flats region of South Africa. Over the past few decades, they have begun saying *I do try to tell her but she won't listen* instead of *I try to tell her but she won't listen, I do see it on Tuesdays* instead of *I see it on Tuesdays.* This is considered a slovenly scourge by schoolteachers in the area, and is in general seen as a linguistic bad habit as alarming and frustrating as Black English's use of *to be* is to educated Americans. Yet to us, if anything, *I do see it on Tuesdays* has a quaint, rather biblical air about it—but black people's *I done seen it Tuesday* is considered "English going to the dogs." If one is okay, then so is the other one, and thus we see that anyone railing against either of them is caught up in the natural mistake of confusing sociological associations with linguistic truth. This little *do* gets up educated South Africans' noses because the people saying it are of humble social class, pure and simple.

Now that we understand that speech that isn't standard is not a degraded version of the standard, we are in a position to understand a final point.

6. *If a person speaks a colloquial dialect, it is not a symptom of an inability to speak a standard one.* On the contrary, around the world, it is quite normal for people to speak both a colloquial and a standard dialect. We know this in a sense, in that many of us are conscious that we talk one way with friends and another way at work or when making a presentation. However, we often have a feeling that the way we speak with friends is a loosening of the standard variety, that we are letting the rules go because it would be hard, and even a little anal, to stand up straight and wear a tie all day long every day. In fact, however, what we are doing when we use colloquial varieties at home is switching from the standard to a different, but similarly complex, system.

If you ask a Swiss German speaker, for example, how to say "Only language gave the foreigner away" in standard German, keeping in mind that the German way of saying it places the main verb at the end, they will give you:

Nur die Sprache hat den Ausländer verraten.
only the language has the foreigner given-away

But in their home language, Swiss German, it would be:

Nu s Muul häd de Ussländer verraate.
only the language has the foreigner given-away

The Swiss version is not "broken down" German, but essentially a different language, which developed separately from standard German and happened not to be the variety chosen as the coin of the realm. A German who moves to Switzerland has to learn Swiss German just as we would, and though it is akin enough to standard German that a German certainly has a head start on us here, even a German will most likely never speak Swiss German identically to native Swiss, and will always be "given away by their speech as foreigners." For Swiss German speakers, Swiss German is not a bad habit to be undone, but an alternative system that they use alongside the standard. This kind of two-layered speech repertoire is quite ordinary worldwide: the Arabic the Egyptian speaks at home is essentially a different language than what they would speak in a classroom; the Italian who says *Chi che t'è vest?* for "Who did you see?" in the kitchen says *Chi hai visto?* when they work in the city; the educated Haitian will say *Mwen te manje* in Haitian Creole for "I ate" at home, but *J'ai mangé* in French at the office, and so on.

In the same way, then, the child who tells her teacher "That girl doesn't bother me anymore" and then tells her mother that night "She don't be messin' wit' me now" is not lapsing into "improper English"—she is using a separate game plan, an alternative grammar, using *be,* and negating it, in a way that many of us would have to carefully master if we were to learn Black English with a cassette set. Just as Swiss have no trouble keeping two tracks in use in their heads, Americans can effortlessly handle both standard and colloquial varieties of English.

"You Don't Speak Properly"

What we have seen in this chapter all comes down to one simple thing that is useful for teachers to keep in mind as they approach the colloquial dialects they hear in America's classrooms: there is no such thing as a native speaker of English speaking bad grammar. Of course, the young child who has yet to master language itself period makes true mistakes: *They goed outside* is indeed a mistake, showing that a child has yet to learn *went,* the irregular past form of *go.* Importantly, however, no adult black or white would say *He goed.* Adults would, however, say things like *I ain't got nothin'* and *They be tellin' the same stories across town,* and things like this are not violations of standard English, but legal, articulate constructions in *other kinds of* English that happen not to have been chosen as standard.

This is in no way a call for students to simply be allowed to speak only colloquial English. Always and forever, the standard variety will be indispensable to upward mobility, and always and forever, one of the main places children acquire comfort and fluency in the standard variety will be in school. When they come to school, children often have only limited ability in the standard variety, because colloquial dialects are the home language and are thus what children learn first. Think about the skits on *In Living Color* when Homey the Clown was assigned to a class of small black children and the actors playing them spontaneously switched into Black English. What we must always recall, however, is that even if the rest of the world is often unaware of this, the job of school is to *add a new layer* to a child's speech repertoire, *not to undo* the one they already have.

Exercises

1. Show your students these three passages from the Prodigal Son parable, written in different stages of English, and discuss the ways in which English has changed over the centuries.

   Old English, 999:
   Sōthlīce his yldra sunu wæs on æcere, and hē cōm, and thā hē thām hūse genēalæhte, he gehyrde thæne swēg and thæt wered. thā clypode hē ānne thēow, and ācsode hine hwæt thæt wære.

Middle English, 1380:
Forsoth his eldere sone was in the feeld, and whanne he cam and neighede to the houe, he herde a symfonye and a croude. And he cleipede oon of the seruantis, and axide what thingis thes weren.

Modern English, 1961:
Now the elder son was out on the farm; and on his way back, as he approached the house, he heard music and dancing. He called one of the servants and asked what it meant.

2. Have students "translate" this passage from the balcony scene in Shakespeare's *Romeo and Juliet* into modern English, encouraging them to use a dictionary to find the meanings of unfamiliar words like *wherefore, thy* and *thee,* and *doff,* and now unfamiliar usages such as that of *wilt* and *owe.*

Juliet:
O Romeo, Romeo! Wherefore art thou Romeo?
Deny thy father and refuse thy name;
Or, if thou wilt not, be but sworn my love,
And I'll no longer be a Capulet.

Romeo:
(Aside) Shall I hear more, or shall I speak at this?

Juliet:
'Tis but thy name that is my enemy;
Thou art thyself, though not a Montague.
What's Montague? It is nor hand, nor foot,
Nor arm, nor face, nor any other part
Belonging to a man. O, be some other name!
What's in a name? That which we call a rose
By any other name would smell as sweet;
So Romeo would, were he not Romeo call'd,
Retain that dear perfection which he owes
Without that title. Romeo, doff thy name,
And for that name which is no part of thee
Take all myself.

3. Ask the students if they feel that they talk just like their parents. If they feel that they do not, then ask them why they talk differently, and where they think the differences may have come from. Finally, ask them if they think these differences are permanent parts of their speech or whether they will only talk this way during their teen and college years.

2

It's Just Slang, Isn't It?

Even if we now understand that colloquial dialects are not linguistic laziness but linguistic variation, there are some lingering areas of discomfort about dialects that we may still reasonably harbor. In this chapter, I will show that the things we saw in the last chapter lead us out of even these honest misconceptions. This will allow us to even more fully understand what we hear around us in the United States and beyond and develop ideas for how to approach such things in the classroom.

What Is Slang?

For one, so far I have necessarily presented an oversimplified concept of what a dialect is. In doing so, I have left unaddressed the deeply felt but ill-defined overlap between dialect and slang in public perception. The two concepts do overlap, to be sure, but in a narrower band than most suppose. Under the general supposition that dialect and slang are more or less the same thing, the intelligent reader may well wonder what all the fuss about dialect is and what it really has to do with classroom teaching. In fact, a more fine-grained sense of the relationship between slang and dialect can open our eyes to classroom issues that may not have been apparent before.

We naturally conflate dialect and slang because when most of us think about what speech consists of, we think of words. When I was little, there was a six-language word list appendix in our large English-language dictionary, and I found this so fascinating that I decided I would use it to write the lyrics to "Twinkle, Twinkle, Little Star" in all six of these languages (for some reason one of them was Yiddish!). My natural misimpression was that to do this all I had to do was plug in the foreign word for each English word; I knew nothing of conjugation, gender agreement, or word order. I had fun doing it (I was that kind of kid), but the results were poetry such as the Spanish rendition: *Centellear, centellear, pequeño estrella / Cómo yo preguntarse qué tu ser . . .*

Now, of course, none of us would pull this as adults, but the story illustrates how natural it is for words to dominate our conception of how we and others talk. We all know intellectually that learning a language also means learning its grammar, and even that this part is actually the most time-consuming and difficult aspect of the process—if all we had to do was memorize lists of words then language-learning classes would barely be worth being called classes. Yet in daily life, when we listen to a different kind of English than our own, we think first of words: "Oh, down there they say 'Carry me to the store' instead of 'Take me to the store.' "

However, words are only one of three main things that make up speech, and when we are dealing with dialect differences, we need to be equally aware of all three. Namely, speech consists of:

1. words
2. sounds
3. sentence structure

Sounds

Words we know, but let's get to the sounds. We all know that speech has sounds. However, as dull as sounds might seem in themselves, they are every bit as important as words when we think about dialect differences, because sounds often *interact* in different ways according to dialect. We can see this first by looking at the starker example of differences in sound interaction between separate languages.

In English, when nouns end in *f*, the *f* often changes to a *v* sound when plural *-s* is added: *leaf* versus *leaves, half* versus *halves*. This feels as natural to us as breathing—we would think of *halfs* as kind of awkward. Yet in German, when you tack an *s* onto the end of a word that ends with *f*, the *f* stays *f*. "Train station" is *Bahnhof* (BONN-hawf); if you say "the train station's roof," you say "the roof of the train station": *Das Dach des Bahnhofs*, where *Bahnhofs* is pronounced "BONN-hawfs," not "BONN-hawves." Thus, it is not that it is the very nature of *f* worldwide to change to a *v* at the end of a word like caterpillars turn into butterflies. *F*'s tendency to do this in English is a trait it happened to take on in our particular language.

In the same way, each *dialect* of *one* language tends to have idiosyncrasies in how its sounds interact. In Black English, the sound *eh* becomes more like *ay-uh* before certain consonants: *m, n, l,* and *d.* Therefore, in Black English the word *bet* sounds pretty much like it does in standard English, but the word *bell* sounds more like "bail," *bed* more like approximately "bay-id." It is these specific sound patterns that make for a perceptible *accent.* Meanwhile, in deep Southern White English *eh* goes to "ay-uh" before any consonant—imagine Gomer Pyle or Forrest Gump saying *bet:* "bay-it." Because the sound interactions in this dialect are slightly different than the ones in Black English, this is a different *accent* from Black English's. Each dialect has its own little kit of such sound interactions, which is why we can distinguish, say, Southern White from Black English even over the phone. However, accent is *only* about sounds: the written words would look standard. Bill Clinton, for example, has a Southern White accent, but one would never know this from written copies of his State of the Union addresses.

Structure

Our third component, *structure,* is as vital a component in speech as words and sounds. What I am calling structure is roughly similar to what most of us would call grammar, but grammar is often associated with "refined" touches like *Billy and I sang* versus *Billy and me sang,* whereas structure refers to the basic things no one is considered to ever "get wrong," such as the fact that in English, adjectives come before nouns—*the good boy,* not *the boy good.*

Again, the importance of structure in thinking about dialects is best illustrated by starting with thinking about separate languages. It is clear to us that languages differ in their structure as well as sounds—Spanish, for example, usually puts its adjectives after the noun instead of before (*una casa blanca* "a white house"); German often puts the verb at the end of the sentence, such that "I knew you visited her yesterday" comes out "I knew that you her yesterday visited." There are even languages where the verb comes first.

Less obvious to us is that even dialects of a single language can differ from one another in terms of basic structure. For example, one regional Italian form for "Who did you see?" is *Chi che t'è vest?,* which word-for-word is "Who that you have seen?" But the standard *Chi hai visto?* is simply "Whom you have seen?"

These three aspects of language are important because speech can differ from a standard variety by degrees according to these levels.

Levels of Difference

Some dialects differ from standard English only in words and set expressions. A good example of this is whatever "teenspeak" of the moment garners media attention. For example, the "Valley Girl" lingo enshrined in a Frank Zappa pop hit and a charming movie in the early 1980s differed from standard English only in words and expressions, like *totally* and *Gag me with a spoon.* In the same way, despite the vibrancy of the lingo in *Clueless*—"Whatever!"— the *sounds* of these teenagers' speech interact in the same ways as the sounds in their teachers' speech, and they are not using different *sentence structures* than their parents. In other words, these dialects, differing from standard speech only in words and set expressions, differ only in terms of *slang.*

On the other hand, where the sound interactions are different from the standard's, we have an *accent.* Thus, if one happened to travel to sandy Okracoke Island off of the coast of North Carolina, one would hear many people saying "hoy toyd" instead of *high tide,* "far" instead of *fire,* and other local sound patterns that make the people there notorious for their "brogue." Alicia Silverstone did not have to master an accent to play Cher in *Clueless;* she simply had to recite lines decorated with a cute slang while wearing pert outfits. However, if she were to venture portraying a local girl from Okracoke, she would have to master this "brogue," a different set of sound interactions.

Finally, even a dialect's basic *structure* can be different from the standard's. Here is where things like the "regularity" *be* of Black English come in. *Be,* although in itself a word, is not just a piece of slang. This is because *be,* unlike *Whatever!,* expresses an underlying grammatical distinction, the indication that something is done on a regular basis. Thus, the likes of *foxy mama* have come and gone among black Americans, but they have been using *be* the way they do for generations. The way this *be* is used is so different from how standard English conveys this area of meaning that it takes careful linguistic analysis to tease out its essence, everyone else mistaking it simply for an unconjugated verb run wild. On the other hand, any of us can pick up *Whatever!* and use it after hearing it perhaps twice. *Whatever!* is leggings; Black English's *be* is a femur—an eternal, fundamental building block of a speech variety's structure.

Generally, these three stages exist in a "stacked" relationship, as shown in Figure 2.1. People who speak with a distinct accent are likely to also have a colorful local slang. This is because they will have developed and then preserved this accent as a result of being relatively isolated from standard speakers, and this kind of isolation naturally leads to the creation of in-group words and expressions in the same way as a tight clique in college develops a battery of in-jokes. The isolation need not be a matter of brute geography as it is with the "hoy toyd" folks living on Okracoke Island. It can also be a subtler but just as powerful social isolation, such as the barriers of culture, history, and class that to this day give Brooklyn the feeling of a separate city from Manhattan, despite its formal incorporation into New York City in 1898.

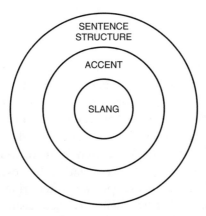

Figure 2.1

In the same way, people whose dialect differs from the standard in terms of structure will also have both an accent as well as their own slang. The paradigm example here is Black English, which differs from standard English to such an extent as the result of a history of uniquely severe isolation from standard speakers, both geographically and sociologically.

Re-examining the Word Around

Understanding these three levels of speech and how they apply to our conception of dialect resolves some areas of confusion that may arise in how we make sense of what we hear around us.

"What About That Bad Accent He Had?" So far I have illustrated the point that dialects that differ down to the structural level, such as the British dialects on pages 4–5 or Black English, are not decayed versions of a standard. Now that we know that dialect also subsumes accent, I can be more precise and point out that accents are not degradations of standard dialects any more than structural differences are. Accents have mostly developed independently of the standard, and in all cases are products of natural change. Something else to keep in mind is that just as colloquial structures are not signs of incomplete learning but of having learned something equal but different, an accent is not a sign of having failed to master the standard accent, but of having simply learned a different accent. In other words, none of us worried that "Valley Talk" was a sign of linguistic sloth or that English was "doomed." In the last chapter I showed that colloquial sentence structures are not interpretable this

way either. Now, we can finesse the point by noting that the same perspective applies to the stage between slang and structure, accent.

"'Ebonics'? My Kids Speak Slang Too, But...." Second, seeing this taxonomy of dialect development allows us to better understand the educators who over the past thirty years have worried that the lag in black students' reading scores may be due to the differences between their home speech and standard English. Many people, including teachers, have been skeptical of such claims, out of a sense that these educators were attempting to attract special treatment to black students on the basis of mere "slang." If these people really were worried that the likes of *Man, that's dope!* were interfering with black students' processing of *The Great Gatsby,* then this skepticism would be justified. However, because dialects differ from the standard to varying degrees, it is too broad an equation to liken Black English to the *Clueless* teenagers' little lingo. Black English, unlike "Valley Talk," is much more than its slang—it is also an accent and a set of local structures.

On the accent—we tend not to think of Black English as involving an accent. We associate the concept of accent with whites, Great Britain, and foreigners. Yet imagine hearing Jesse Jackson on the radio reading the first page of *Pride and Prejudice.* Even when reading standard English written without the slightest hint of ethnic or colloquial flavor (that's why I chose Jane Austen), we would all know, often before the end of the first sentence, that the person reading was African-American. This is because the sound interactions in Jesse Jackson's speech are those of Black English. "It is a truth universally acknowledged," he would begin, "that a single man ("may-in") in possession of a good fortune must ("mus'") be in want of a wife (rather like "wahf")." What we all process as "a black sound" is in fact nothing more or less than an accent.

In the same vein, even apart from its slang and the accent, Black English has its own structures. Here, for example, is a passage in Black English. There is not a bit of slang in it, and we can't hear the reader and so the accent is hidden, and yet this could be no one but a black girl:

> It a girl name Shirley Jones live in Washington. Most everybody on her street like her, 'cause she a nice girl. Shirley treat all of them just like they was her sister and brother, but most of all she like one boy name Charles. But Shirley keep away from Charles most of the time, 'cause she start to liking him so much she be scared of him. So Charles, he don't hardly say nothing to her neither. Still, that girl got to go 'round telling everybody Charles s'posed to be liking her.

The concern that African-American chidren may have special needs in the classroom, then, is based on Black English's *accent* (the difference between *must* and *mus'*) and its sentence structure (that is, what makes the preceding passage immediately identifiable as black speech), not its *slang.*

Slang in the Classroom? The preceding example relates to the final reason this three-tiered conception of dialects is important—it helps us to avoid the natural tendency to think of dialect differences in general as being simply a matter of different groups of people having their own little collections of words. Many discussions of topics like this leave the distinction between slang and dialect hazy, giving as much attention to the former as to the latter. The problem here is that the idea that colloquial accents and colloquial structure differences are not decay runs so counter to what we are trained to think that it may be tempting to think "Sure, there's nothing wrong with all their cute slang, but we still need to get rid of their bad grammar."

What we are seeing here, however, is that slang is merely the beginning of a continuum that proceeds through accent on to sentence structure, with all three being both inevitable and harmless. This general process is a response to geographical and social separation, which makes two varieties of a language change in as many different directions as the same ones. The extent to which the change proceeds depends on the extent of the separation. Separated by the expanse of a continent, French people and Romanians turned Latin into two whole new languages. Separated by concentration in one region and centuries of oppression, Black Americans developed their own sentence structures, accent, and slang. Separated from Manhattan by the East River, a municipal administration, and intense local pride, Brooklynites developed an accent and a slang. Separated from their parents by a bedroom wall and adolescent ennui, California teenagers developed a slang and started saying *Whatever!*

All of these things fall at various points on a continuum: just as water can be lukewarm, hot, or boiling, dialects differ from the standard to varying degrees. Of course, there are no distinct dividing lines here anymore than there are with water along the way to boiling. As accents go, the Minnesota accent popularized by the *Fargo* characters is only slightly different from standard English compared to the accent of the characters in *Goodfellas,* whereas the speech of people off the coast of North Carolina with a thick "brogue" can take a little while to quite wrap your ears around. Brooklynese is largely a matter of accent, but does have the occasional sentence structure that is different from standard English's (*There ain't nothin' here*). Both the accent and sentence structures of Jamaican speech are so different from standard English that Jamaican patois is virtually incomprehensible to the uninitiated, and tempts classification as a different language altogether. What this means is that there is no logical point along this continuum where it makes sense to call "Foul!"—if no one sees the impending fall of Anglophone civilization in Alicia Silverstone on her cell phone saying *Whatever!,* then the language will also be just fine if someone in a bar in Cincinnati says *Ain't got none.*

"Lazy Tongues"

The accent issue bears a bit more discussion. One aspect of colloquial accents that often gives them the appearance of being evidence of "lazy tongues" is that often their particular sounds seem to be less complex versions of their equivalents in standard dialects. Hearing *dem, dese,* and *dose* and seeing *them, these,* and *those* written down, we often wonder "Why can't these people stick their tongues between their teeth and say *th* instead of just being satisfied with *d?*" We might wonder "How can these dialects really be equal to the standard when their sounds always seem to involve relaxations, or eliminations, of standard sounds?"

For one, in point of fact colloquial dialects often have sounds that are more complex than standard equivalents. This doesn't occur to us because we are trained to think of any difference from the standard in a colloquial dialect as a *mis*pronunciation rather than as an *alternative* pronunciation, which distracts us from even considering that the colloquial sound might actually be quirkier than the standard one. An example is the way many Brooklynites pronounce *p, t,* or *k,* especially at the beginning of a stressed syllable. This is a subtle distinction difficult to convey on paper, but to get a sense of it, say *karma* and then say *key.* Notice that the *k* in *key* is a little tenser, has a bit more of a "click" in it, than the one in *karma.* Now say *karma* using the *k* you used in *key.* And now think about the way you imagine Joe Pesci would say *karma,* with a cocky sort of "flip" on the *k*— if you think about it, this is part of what makes up the Brooklyn accent. (If you ever saw Judd Hirsch of *Taxi*'s second sitcom *Dear John,* recall the way the street-corner smart-aleck Kirk would cockily spit out his name when introducing himself, rather like "Gkirk!") That's a tricky sound to imitate, and that's because it's a quirkier sound than standard English's boring *k* sound.

Now think about how seldom you hear anyone but a black person do a really good imitation of black speech. There are plenty of gifted white mimics who can bring an Irish person, a Brooklynite, a Russian, or a Frenchman into the room, but almost all of them slip when trying to do a black person, and would be helpless if they had to do it without the distracting addition of gestures, body language, slang, etc. The supertalented voice artists on *The*

Old Eng ⟩
Middle Engl.

Simpsons could manage only the lamest of Bill Cosbys, Tracey Ullman tries to do a black woman and is entertaining, but nowhere near as spot-on as she is doing anyone else. This is because especially the vowels in Black English are a subtle, complex business. I have said that *bell* sounds more like *bail* in Black English, but it's not *quite* like *bail*—to try to mimic black speech by simply saying *Ring dem bails* for *Ring those bells* sounds exaggerated and more deep Southern white than black. Except in rare cases, one has to grow up speaking Black English to pull off its sound, and that is because its sound system is more complex in many ways than standard English's is.

However, to the extent that colloquial sounds are simpler than standard sounds, we must see this in the perspective of our basic tenet that language always changes. Because the standard is frozen on the page and taught that way to generation after generation, it changes more slowly than colloquial dialects do. From about 1000 A.D. to 1300, English changed from Old English, a bizarre foreign tongue to us, to Middle English, which looks to us like our own language in a fun house mirror. Since then, however, it has changed less—the language of Shakespeare, who started writing in the late 1500s, is a challenge for us but is obviously essentially "what we speak." This is because the invention of printing enshrined standard English on the page (and created the illusion that a language is not supposed to change). In the meantime, however, colloquial dialects are not enshrined on paper and not taught in school alongside math and science. Therefore, they are free to change relatively freely, and they do.

Interesting // /

What this means is that colloquial dialects are often further along on natural paths of change than standards, which are artificially held back by printing and school, just as medicine and hygiene artificially hold humans back from natural evolution while other animals are still out there developing into new species. We saw that one way sounds change is to become simpler. In this light, *th* is a weird little sound that does not occur in very many of the world's languages—of the languages we tend to learn, only Spanish has it and then only in Spain itself—and wherever it appears it is always particularly ripe for evolving into something else. It is therefore exactly what we would expect that the standard variety still has *them, these,* and *those* while the mark of almost any self-respecting colloquial dialect is to have *dem, dese,* and *dose.* The colloquial dialects are actually the advanced ones, moving along while the standard is constipated into holding on to things nobody really wants!

But then recall that another way sounds change is to develop into pricklier ones. Prickly old *th* got into English that way, starting as good old *t,* and this is how *Gkirk* and *bails* got into colloquial dialects we hear in the United States. It is hard to shake the idea that if left to go on their merry way, such dialects would just wear down to nubs, but in fact they would maintain the same balance of simplicity and complexity that all human speech varieties do—because this is exactly how all of the varieties of all of the world's languages, both standard and colloquial, have arisen. The same Black English speaker who says *lef'* instead of *left* is also using a vowel in the word *bell* that even a Tracey Ullman cannot precisely imitate.

Grammar Versus Logic

Another thing about language that bears looking at when we think about dialects is a sense we tend to have that language should follow the rules of formal logic.

Double Negatives

In English dialects, this colors our judgements especially in the notorious case of double negatives like *I don't see nothin'*. We are taught that this is a mistake because two negatives equal a positive, such that *I don't see nothin'* properly means "It is not nothing that I see", and thus "I see something". However, although we might like it to, language simply does not hew perfectly to the rules of formal logic. Of course, it largely does, or communication would be impossible. But like everything in nature, language has its shaggy edges. House cats feel a bizarre need to knead things with their claws and circle a few times before settling into repose, for example. Whatever purpose this served their ancestors in the wild, this is a senseless bit of business in cats' lives now. As brilliantly engineered as they are in most other ways (watch a cat grab a fly out of the air), in the modern house cat, this is an imperfection, a queer little excresence, a tic. Languages are similar when it comes to logic.

For one thing, in the true sense double negatives are not illogical in terms of comprehension, because we instantly know perfectly well what a person means when they say *I don't see nothin'*. We do not stop to wonder whether they mean "I see something," even if we never use the construction ourselves and first hear it coming from someone else during our childhood. No child hears this said and asks their mother what the person sees. On the contrary, it has to be carefully explained to us *how* this is illogical!

Besides this, even standard English has lapses of logic that we rarely even notice. *I'm on this side, aren't I?* Surely nothing wrong here—but then if you say *I am,* then shouldn't it be *amn't I?* This is not logical, but no one complains. Remember that *you* started out as a plural word only. As people started using *you* for one person, there were people standing around saying it was illogical, and I suppose it was. But we're here, they're dead, and, well, language just isn't strictly logical. When's the last time you heard a French teacher sigh that *Comment allez-vous?* "How are you" was illogical because *vous,* like *you,* started out as a plural word?

More to the point, however, double negatives are the *only* way to express the negative in a great many languages, even in their most formal speech. For example, to say "I don't see anything" in French one says *Je ne vois rien,* word for word "I not see nothing." Yet no French person is told that *Je ne vois rien* is illogical—on the contrary, in colloquial French the first negative word *ne* is dropped (*Je vois rien*) but this is considered "bad" French, evidence that the language is "going to the dogs"! The French are notoriously proud of their language, one pedant having even gone so far as to say "What isn't clear isn't French" (*Ce qui n'est pas clair n'est pas français*). If they can feel this way despite flouting the rules of formal logic about once a minute, then surely we can give colloquial English speakers a break here. This is especially true given that double negation of this kind is par for the course all over the world, in Spanish, Russian, Hebrew, Japanese, and thousands of other languages: *Don Quixote, Anna Karenina,* Kabuki plays, and even the original Hebrew Bible are all dripping with double negatives. Unless we are prepared to condemn all of these mighty works as written in bad grammar, we see that the idea that colloquial English double negatives are bad grammar is an illusion. Why would it be bad grammar in English but okay in the Bible?

To Be or Not To Be

A related example is the absence of the verb *to be* in certain sentences in Black English. Under the idea that language must follow the rules of formal logic, a sentence like *She my sister* certainly appears "broken"—after all, don't we need to indicate the relationship of equation between *she* and *my sister* to have a full sentence? It was actually proposed in the 1960s that sentences like this were an indication of genuine cognitive deficiency among black American children.

Yet in fact, if a sentence like *She my sister* is evidence of cognitive deficiency, then Anton Chekhov must have been something of a moron, and the writers of the Bible must have been *idiots savants.* This is because it is extremely common in languages around the world to not have a verb *to be* in sentences meaning *she is my sister, she is in the tree,* or *she is tall.*

In this scene from Chekhov's play *The Cherry Orchard,* for example, the grande dame actress Lyubov Andreev is having a tense exchange with the moony student Trofimov. Trofimov makes the mistake of laying it out to her that her faithless lover in Paris was a "dog," as we might say today. (The *j*'s stand for the sound of *y;* the *y* stands for a strange sound in Russian rather like the sound Lucille Ball would turn to the camera and make before a fade-out when she was in trouble with Ricky on *I Love Lucy*—say "uh" and then almost close your teeth together.)

On mjelkij negodjai, nichtozjestvo . . .
he   petty   rascal   nonentity

"He's a little cad, a piece of nothing . . ."

She comes back by throwing at him that at twenty-six, he is still just a poor student:

. . . a vy vsjo jeshchjo gimnazist vtorovo klassa!
and you all still   student   second   class

". . . and here you are still just a college student!"

Note that there are no *be*'s here—"He a little cad," "You still just a student." As you see, an inner-city black American would be quite at home with these sentences (although *cad* would not be quite the *mot juste*, of course), and yet this is high Russian. These characters are cultivated, educated people—they are on a country estate, not a street corner. They are not "dropping" *be*—they are using standard Russian grammar, which happens to be one that usually conveys the relationship of being via inference. Certainly Russian is not an illogical language—we don't suppose that Mikhail Gorbachev would have been more likely to hold on to power if he used a verb *to be* more often.

Some languages are like this, some aren't—it's largely a matter of chance. Much of our impression that a language has to have a *be* in sentences like this in order to make sense is due to the accidental fact that most of the foreign languages we tend to learn—French, Spanish, Italian, German—happen to use their *to be* as consistently as English does. The impression, however, is merely accidental. If we have occasion to cast our net wider than these old chestnuts, as often as not we have to unlearn *to be* in many basic sentences: Arabic, Hungarian, Indonesian, and on and on.

We are hardly unique in our sense of this; for anyone who happens to use a *be* across the board, it inevitably looks weird for a language not to. Czech is closely related to Russian and the languages have very similar grammars, but Czech never omits the verb *to be*. Once I told a Czech speaker that Russians say "she my sister" where Czech says "she is my sister" and her response was "That's stupid!" which it must have seemed from her perspective, speaking English and Czech, which both use a *to be* all of the time. But the fact that Russian can do without *to be* while Czech, similar enough for some mutual intelligibility, craves it, leads us to the fact that even dialects of the same language can differ on *to be*. That is what we see in Black English and standard English. Maybe it's no accident that whites have picked up black Americans'

You de man, because it's right there in the original Hebrew text of the Bible (2 Samuel 12:7)—*Atah ha-eesh,* quite literally "You the man" to mean "You are the man." In not bothering itself with a pesky little word that context can take care of anyway, Black English is not illogical, it's *Biblical!*

Complexity: A Relative Term

A guiding concept I have tried to get across is that when it comes to language, as with so much else, there is hidden complexity in the humble. To finesse our sense of this further, it is useful to pull the camera back and see how English in general compares to other languages on this score. As languages go, English is in fact a pretty bread-and-butter business even in its most elaborated forms.

Written Versus Spoken

For example, it is true that written English can achieve a complexity of arrangement that is almost never encountered in speech, because writing allows careful forethought and reading allows time for decoding, whereas hearing speech allows neither. For example, in writing we can say:

> After having seen the whole movie, feeling relatively unwilling to reveal her private opinion about something the director had obviously put so much work into on a shoestring budget, she decided to pretend she had liked it in order to save his feelings.

Because almost all writing is in standard English, standard English gets to flex its muscles in clause sandwiches like this while colloquial dialects do not, although if colloquial dialects happened to have been chosen as standards, then they could have been used in similar kinds of sentences. After all, standard English only got to sit in the shop window by accident.

Yet it bears mentioning that in many other languages, ordinary written usage is even more baroque than anything we could imagine in standard English. For example, in Mikhail Bulgakov's novel *The Master and Margarita,* one descriptive passage has been translated into English as:

> A haze of smoke was drifting towards the arcade across the upper courtyard of the garden, coming from the wing at the rear of the palace, the quarters of the first cohort of the XII legion; known as the "Lightning," it had been stationed in Jerusalem since the Procurator's arrival.

Pretty ordinary stuff for us. But in Russian, word by word, the passage is:

> From the wing at the rear of the palace, where lodged themselves the having-come with the Procurator to Jerusalem first cohort of the

Twelfth Lightning legion, drifted smoke towards the colonnade across the upper courtyard of the garden.

Notice how much Russian can pack into that one tapeworm "the having-come with the Procurator to Jerusalem first cohort of the Twelfth Lightning legion"—we have to strain to wrap our heads around so much being put before the noun, and the translator has to split this information across two clauses. The thing is that this is quite ordinary for written Russian; this comes from a novel that occupies about the same place in Russian society that *The Great Gatsby* does for us. It's just one book of millions; the reading Russian whizzes right by sentences like this the way we do sentences like the English one about the movie. Written German is very similar.

Complexity in Unexpected Places

The most useful thing for us to keep in mind, though, is that in other languages, even *casual* speech is far more complex than anything we can even imagine. One example is Ojibwe (oh-JIB-way), a language spoken by Native Americans in the Great Lakes region (roll Ojibwe around in your mouth and you get Chippewa, the "Euro" name for the group). Ojibwe has several words for many things that we consider too basic to even imagine needing more than one word for. For example, there is a different word for *break* depending not on how you break something—even we have *shatter, wrench, mash*—but on *what* you break. If you broke a stick you *bookw* (BOAKW) it, if you broke a string you *bak* (BOCK) it, if you broke a three-dimensional object you *baashk* (BOSHK) it. However, even these words you can't just use by themselves; you have to also tack on a piece specifying *how* you broke something. For example, if you stepped on or sat on a stick, you *book**shk*** it. Sometimes this little piece is just one little sound, but not anything we even think of as a "sound": the catch in the throat we really make for *t* when we say *cotton*. Thus, if we broke a balloon with some instrument, then we follow *baashk* with something rather like a quick reversed hiccup. On top of this, you have to say "I broke *it* the balloon"; just "I broke the balloon" is as incomplete in Ojibwe as *We not swim* instead of *We do not swim* would be to us. Thus "I broke a balloon," with ' being the reversed hiccup, is:

Ngii-baashk' -aan ombaasjigan.
I   break with it   balloon

The amazing thing is that adding these pieces specifying how the breaking was done is not a matter of *precise* or *refined* language the way deciding to say *shatter* instead of *break* is for us—you *have* to say it this way.

By the way, I am oversimplifying in saying that *baashk'* is a "word"; the dashes in the example are how linguists show that the whole *ngiibaashk'aan* is one word, which all goes by as fast as we say *qualification*. But if you want to say that you set in motion a series of events that ended in the balloon being popped, such as angrily overturning a chair that hit a shelf with an axe on it that fell onto the balloon and popped it, then you have to tack on not the reverse hiccup, but a different ending *shkood* (SHKOAD):

Ngii-baashk-shkood-		oon	ombaasjigan.
I	break	unintentionally it	balloon

Finally, if you knocked the chair over by accident rather than deliberately, then you need in addition a special prefix *bchi-*, such that there is one whole word *ngiibchibaashkshkoodoon* to express what we need eight words for, "I made the balloon get popped by accident":

Ngii-bchi-	baashk-shkood-		oon	ombaasjigan.
I	by accident break	unintentionally it	balloon	

Oh yeah—there is no *a* or *the* in Ojibwe; the way you would say that you broke *a* balloon instead of *the* balloon is to put *balloon* first, such that "I made *a* balloon get popped by accident" is:

Ombaasjigan	ngii-bchi-	baashk-shkood-		oon.
balloon	I	by accident break	unintentionally it	

And these are only some of the words for *break,* and *break* is only one of several verbs that differ this way depending on what they affect. In all kinds of ways Ojibwe makes explicit differentiations of things that would never occur to us as even requiring acknowledgment in speech—to an Ojibwe, English looks "sloppy" for not distinguishing between these kinds of breaking, and not having to indicate whether it was intentional or not. And look at these sounds—we've got our little *th,* but nothing like this hiccuping in reverse not just after vowels like in our *cotton,* but after consonants too—try saying "*baashk*-(reverse hiccup)" *fast!* In being tied so finely to experience, having a more complex sound system, and bristling with an array of prefixes and endings that make English look like a storm blew off its clothes, Ojibwe is so complex that children do not learn to speak it completely until the age of ten. Many Native American languages are this complex, including the Eskimo (today, Inuit) languages.

What all of this shows is that speech varieties vary on a continuum of overall complexity, but rich communication is possible through all of them. What drives this home for us is that even standard English itself is only middling in terms of how many linguistic bells and whistles humans can handle worldwide. Ordinary conversations among the hunter-gatherer Ojibwes Europeans met in the 1600s were more elaborate than anything we even do on paper, and yet we do not consider English primitive. In the same way, there is nothing inherently "second-drawer" about colloquial English dialects, especially because they contain many hidden complexities of their own.

Communication Gaps

Seeing that colloquial dialects are alternatives rather than violations finally shows us that what can appear to be someone's failure to communicate—and often even rudeness—often results from what is in fact a simple lack of fit between two legitimate but different dialects.

Wish I May, Wish I Might

To any American, for example, there are two possible interpretations of *may* in this sentence:

> You may run all the way to the post office, but I'm sure it will be closed by the time you get there.

One interpretation, and probably the first one that comes to most of our minds, is that *may* means "might." Under this interpretation, the sentence means that no matter what approach you take to getting the letter to the post office, one of which might be that you run the whole way, you're out of luck.

The other interpretation is that *may* means "are allowed to," and that the person is giving the other one permission to run to the post office. *May* in American English has both of these meanings, with context directing our interpretation of its meaning in any given sentence.

However, an English speaker in India would only process this sentence with the "permission" interpretation; the first one, the most natural to us, would never occur to them because *may* simply does not have the "might" meaning in Indian English. Importantly, by "Indian English" I do not mean English learned in school as a second language like we learn French and Spanish, such that the issue here would be that the people have yet to pick up the "might" meaning. Indian English refers to the full English spoken by even the most educated Indians, often learned during childhood along with Hindi and other native Indian languages. Over the centuries, millions of Indians have used English as the language of everyday communication, but because this usage has taken place apart from the English being spoken in Great Britain and the United States, it has slowly developed a number of conventions of its own just as colloquial dialects within Great Britain and the United States have. The result is a standard Indian English, quite recognizable to us, but with various departures from what we think of as English.

This of course includes vocabulary, but also, as we would predict based on what we have seen in this book, accent and even structure as well. One can imagine the possibilities of misunderstanding between these dialects given things like this *may* mismatch. Surely, the effect on trade relations between India and the United States is slight, but an Indian might quietly wonder as they were hoofing it off to the post office why the person they were talking to considered permission a part of the equation.

The Hads and the Had-Nots

There are similar little mismatches between standard English and Black English. When I was little, I remember being vaguely confused by the way my cousins used *had* in telling stories: "And I had gone down the block to see where she was and she had hid around the corner and I had said 'Where she at?' and then she had come bustin' out before I could catch her . . ." For a standard English speaker, this use of *had* sounds like the pluperfect, indicating that something took place before the past time being referred to in the story, in the "past-before-the-past." What I was waiting for was something like "And I had gone down the block to see where she was, and then she hid around the corner and I said 'Where she at?' . . . ," where the narrator uses his having gone around the block as a quick piece of background but then gets back to the heart of the narration and sets it in the regular past. This is how the pluperfect is used in standard English, as a scene-setter for something that happened in the past or to indicate the cause of something that happened in the past: *I had already seen the photos, so I went to the kitchen to get a Coke.*

But my cousins would pile *had* upon *had* like this without ever settling back into the regular past—the *hads* followed one another fast and furiously right to the end of the story. To me, it seemed like my cousins had trouble quite getting to a point, and when they were done I always wondered why they were stopping before the end. Because they had usually finished with some grand climax, I, caught up in their excitement and assuming that everything they had said was the prelude to something else, ended up wondering what truly smashing thing had followed the "appetizer" they had given me, and why they had denied me the payoff.

What this was, however, was a different usage of *had* specific to Black English. While standard English uses *had* for the pluperfect, in narrations Black English uses it as a marker of *regular* past. Therefore the *had*'s my cousins used were not meant to set a scene or explain causes: the sentences with *had* were not preludes to the real story—they *were* the real story itself.

Related speech varieties differ in how they use their *have*'s: the French speaker says "I have seen" (*J'ai vu*) to express not what we would say as "I have seen" but as the simple past "I saw," but in Spanish "I have seen" (*He visto*) means just what it does for us, for example. This different meaning of *had* in Black English can be very confusing to non-speakers, even someone like me who grew up not speaking the dialect but hearing it used in context quite a bit.

Singing Our Songs

Other cross-dialectal misinterpretations can come from an aspect of dialects I have so far made little mention of: intonation or melody, an aspect of a speech variety's sound system. Intonation feels to us like a marginal aspect of communication, partly because we do not indicate it in writing, but it is often nothing less than <u>central in conveying meaning.</u> An example: someone sees paintings hanging on your walls and says "Who's the artist?" The neutral interpretation of the sentence is that the person is asking who painted the paintings, expecting to be told that it was a local talent. However, there is a way of uttering the sentence that would immediately convey that the asker assumes that the artist is you or someone else living in the house; namely, low pitches on "Who's the" and a sharply higher pitch on the first syllable of "artist"—*Who's the AR-tist?* The thing is that things like this vary from one dialect to another. For example, a British person might not catch that "Who's the AR-tist?" means "Did you or your daughter paint these?" because this little intonation pattern does not have this meaning in British English.

I once saw intonation create one of these miscues on television during the Tony Awards for theatre. Nell Carter, the African-American actress and singer, announced that the winner for best costumes that year was the late Patricia Zipprodt, and then called "Patricia?" as Zipprodt approached the podium. Carter called her name with a certain intonation pattern local to black culture impossible to indicate on paper, tinging a summons with a slight hint of playful challenge. This intonation pattern on a name connotes intimacy; what <u>Carter was</u> saying in effect was "<u>Get on up here, girlfriend,</u>" striking a note <u>of professional camaraderie.</u> Zipprodt, however, did not happen to be of a sort likely to cue in to subtle aspects of black speech like this. Carter stood visibly waiting for eye contact and a hug, but Zipprodt walked right up to the podium with no acknowledgment of the note Carter was trying to strike. Zipprodt was probably not a rude or cold person; she simply did not know what this very particular "Patricia" meant, and probably processed it as a rather redundant and perhaps even pushy repetition of her name.

In classrooms, black children have been similarly misinterpreted innocently when a teacher asked them a question and they said *I don't know* with a high pitch on *know*: "I don' KNOW . . ." Within black culture, that use of pitch means that the child is willing to cooperate but wants a hint or some encouragement, like a dog rolling over for a pat on the belly. The child simply opting out would put the high pitch on *don't,* often abbreviated to a mere *uh,* and then land the *know* on a pitch between the low one of *I* and the high one of *don't*—"I UH know." White teachers, however, have sometimes missed the meaning of this intonation difference between standard and Black English and assumed that black students were being uncooperative.

Thus, just as dialects differ according to words, sound interactions, and sentence structures, they are also founded upon similar but slightly divergent intonation patterns that can cause confusion. We can minimize such misfires by being aware of their possibility.

The general point of this chapter has been to take a closer look at dialects and clear up some common and natural misconceptions about them. The upshot is that all of us are talking just fine—the Ojibwe, Ann Landers, Tony Danza, Ice Cube. The funny feeling we might get when the list gets to Tony Danza and Ice Cube abates when we remember the other things we have seen. The fact that Danza's "Angela, there ain't nothin' in here!" has two negatives, which would come out as a positive in a math problem, is of no more importance than the fact that a penguin's covering looks like a tuxedo. Ice Cube's *kep'* instead of *kept* is a sign that his speech is not "lazy" but evolved, in the same way that *heaven* evolved from *heofon.* And finally, we now also know that language variation in the United States is much deeper—and ultimately more interesting—than just different lingos in different neighborhoods. America is a melting pot of different varieties of English that all express the full humanity of their speakers, some just slang, some accents, some having their own structures, some melting into each other (standard English is gradually overcoming Brooklynese) and some thriving (Black English is developing new sounds, structures, and slang as you read this), all together making up what in broad view is called "English." Our job is to learn to build bridges between all of these varieties, and the first step is to realize that none of them are bad grammar.

Exercises

1. Here are some passages in standard English translated into nonstandard dialects that are not usually written. Have the students read these passages out loud, with the aim of giving them a sense of how all dialects are equally suitable for expressing thoughts.

THE GOSPEL OF ST. JOHN, CHAPTER 3

Standard English:

Now there was a man of the Pharisees, named Nicodemus, a ruler of the Jews. This came to Jesus by night and said to him, "Rabbi, we know that you are a teacher come from God; for no one can do those signs that you do, unless God is with him." Jesus answered him, "Truly, truly, I say to you, unless one is born anew, he cannot see the kingdom of God." Nicodemus said to him, "How can a man be born when he is old? Can he enter a second time into his mother's womb and be born?"

Black English:

It was a man name Nicodemus. He was a leader of the Jews. This man, he come to Jesus in the night and say, "Rabbi, we know you a teacher that come from God, 'cause can't nobody do the things you be doing 'cept he got God with him." Jesus, he tell him say, "This ain't no jive, if a man ain't born over again, ain't no way he gonna get to know God." Then Nicodemus, he ask him, "How a man gonna be born when he already old? Can't nobody go back inside his mother and get born."

FROM *MAX AND MORITZ*, ORIGINALLY WRITTEN IN GERMAN BY WILHELM BUSCH

Standard English (translation from German by Elly Miller):

As has frequently been stated
People must be educated.
Not alone the A,B,C,
Heightens man's humanity;
Not just simply reading, writing,
Makes a person more inviting;
Nor does Arithmetic learning
Make a pupil more discerning.
Reason, Wisdom, Moral Thought
Must be equally well taught;
And to teach with erudition
Was Professor Lample's mission.

Jamaican Patois (translation by Jean D'Costa):

Ole-time people mek wan rule:
'Learn and study while in school!'
ABC kyan ongle staat
Lov a knallidge in de haat:
Readin', writin' ritmetick
Kyan gi Sietan wan good lick,

Higle smaddy wid no fait
Fine demself a Debbil gate;
Show respeck an lov de wise:
Solomon wi gi yuh prize!
Stody ow fi ondastan
All de ways a Gad an man.
In all learnin', Teacha Lampel
Set de very bes example.

(*Ongle*—only; *gi*—give; *Sietan*—Satan; *higle*—idle; *smaddy*—person [from *somebody*]; *ow*—all; *fi*—to)

Scots English (translation by J. K. Annand):

It was statute and decreed
Whatna learnin Man was need
No alane the ABC
Helps him heicher things comprie;
No alane can scrievin, readin,
Gie the gumption that he's needin;
No alane wi sign and nummer
Should a man his mind encummer
But tak pleisure in acquirin
Gift o Wisdom to inspire'm.
Wi sic thinkin aye to hand
Dominie Duncan took his stand.

(*heicher*—higher; *comprie*—understand; *scrievin*—writing; *gie*—give; *sic*—such)

2. Have students "translate" this passage into standard English, and to discuss what might get "lost" in the translation.

It a girl name Shirley Jones live in Washington. Most everybody on her street like her, 'cause she a nice girl. Shirley treat all of them just like they was her sister and brother, but most of all she like one boy name Charles. But Shirley keep away from Charles most of the time, 'cause she start to liking him so much she be scared of him. So Charles, he don't hardly say nothing to her neither. Still, that girl got to go 'round telling everybody Charles s'posed to be liking her.

But when Valentine Day start to come 'round, Shirley get to worrying. She worried 'cause she know the rest of them girls all going to get Valentine cards from they boyfriends. That Shirley, she so worried, she just don't want to be with nobody.

When Shirley get home, her mother say it a letter for her on the table. Right away Shirley start to wondering who it could be from, 'cause she know don' nobody s'posed to be sending her no kind of letter. So

Shirley, she open the envelope up. And when she do, she can see it's a Valentine card inside, and she see it have Charles name wrote on the bottom.

So now everything going be all right for Shirley, 'cause what she been telling everybody 'bout Charles being her boyfriend ain't no story after all. It done come true!

Then, if there are a lot of African-American students in the class, try having them translate this passage from *The Catcher in the Rye* into Black English!

We always had the same meal on Saturday nights at Pencey. It was supposed to be a big deal, because they gave you steak. I'll bet a thousand bucks the reason they did that was because a lot of guys' parents came up to school on Sunday, and old Thurmer probably figured everybody's mother would ask their darling boy what he had for dinner last night, and he'd say, "Steak." What a racket. You should've seen the steaks. They were these little hard, dry jobs that you could hardly even cut.

3. Each student should watch two hours of television (what drudgery!), each half-hour on a different channel, and note the different dialects that they hear spoken (teenspeak, Black, upper-class British, colloquial British, and even foreign accents) and list three features of the dialect (slang, accent, or sentence structure). Particularly useful programs as of the year 2000 will be *The Simpsons, Sesame Street, The Nanny, E.R.,* and *South Park.*

3

"They Just Mix Them Up!"

In France they speak French. In Russia they speak Russian. In Vietnam they speak Vietnamese. Paging through an almanac, browsing in the encyclopedia, or reading the news, we see that each country has its language. A lot of us know that some countries have more than one—Switzerland has French, German, Italian, and the "other" one Romansh, Belgium has French and Flemish. Given that there are today 192 countries, and that a National Geographic perspective suggests that most countries have one language and some have a few more, we might suppose that there were about 250 languages spoken on earth. Yet there are about *5000* languages distributed among these 192 countries.

If the languages were evenly distributed, each country would contain about twenty-five different languages. Of course this isn't true—there are not twenty-five languages being spoken and passed on to children in Japan, France, or the United States (although immigration transplants many languages from one country to the other). If many countries only have one or two languages, however, it means that others must "take up the slack" to account for 5000, and they do indeed. India is home to 150 languages, Nigeria to 250, and Papua New Guinea—just one half of the island of New Guinea—to about 800, many only spoken by groups of a few hundred.

This means that languages are constantly in contact with one another, like bees in a hive. The solid black borders on a map of the world make it look like each country is home to a language or two kept separate from those beyond its borders except for the occasional person who becomes bilingual by emigrating or being a diplomat. Yet just as it is inherent to languages to change, it has always been inherent for languages to rub constantly up against one another because of their sheer number on this small planet.

This is important for us because this kind of contact creates new dialects and new languages just as language change does. Contact between two languages results in one of them, if not both, being forever altered as a result of the encounter. Just as we often have ambivalent feelings about colloquial dialects because of a sense that the standard dialect is "the language," the symptoms of language contact can look to us like degradations instead of natural transformations. It takes a global perspective to reveal that language mixture is like the blending of colors—ordinary, harmless, marvelous.

Code-Switching

One way that languages rub elbows is that speakers of one language come to dominate speakers of another politically. That, of course, is a sanitized way of saying that big powers annex others through imperialism. Just as imperialism has broadly predictable cultural results, it has broadly predictable linguistic results: a significant number of the imperialized group come to speak the language of the dominant power in addition to their own. This is sparked especially as the dominant power makes its language the vehicle of education and government. This is but one part of a general process whereby the dominant culture is annexed to the old one and becomes part of a new hybrid cultural identity. Thus, the educated Senegalese in Dakar speak French as an official language at work and the African language Wolof at home and with friends, feeling both languages as theirs; the Catalonian in Barcelona will make public statements in Spanish and speak Catalan over dinner.

It is no accident that the dominant language is so often one of a certain European few: English, French, Spanish, Portuguese, or Dutch. These powers colonized most of the world during the slave trade from the late 1400s through the late 1800s and left in their wake a welter of Third World nations where the urban soul splits the difference between English, French, Spanish, Portuguese, or Dutch and any number of local languages. Yet these Western Europeans were not alone in this kind of linguistic colonization. Russian lords it over about 80 languages in the same way, having spread eastward with the Russian Empire; the Chinese have not always been as self-contained as they are now and millennia ago left a profound linguistic imprint on languages southward and eastward; many African languages are spoken along with Arabic as the result of the spread of Islam.

A typical result of this kind of bilingual identity is for people to spontaneously switch between the two languages while conversing; this is called code-switching. Often, one can trace a rough correlation between language and topic, with the dominant language used more often to discuss things like school, politics, and other subjects most likely to have been first encountered in it, whereas the local language is used mostly to talk about casual, intimate, or cultural things. In other situations, there is no particular correlation between language and subject, and the switching is relatively random. Other situations fall somewhere in between, with the local language more often used to convey emotion than the dominant one.

Latino Code-Switching

The code-switching situation we are most familiar with in America is between English and Spanish, heard most among Puerto Ricans in New York and other big cities, and among Mexicans in California and along the Southwestern border. Here, for example, is a Mexican-American (Chicana) woman talking about smoking:

> And they tell me, "How did you quit, Mary?" I didn't quit. I just stopped.
> I mean it wasn't an effort that I made. **Que voy a dejar de fumar porque**
> that I'm going to stop smoking because
>
> **me hace daño o** this or that, uh-uh. It's just that . . . I used to pull butts
> it's bad for me or
>
> out of the wastepaper basket, yeah. **Se me acababan los cigarros en**
> I would run out of cigarettes in
>
> **la noche.** I'd get desperate, **y ahí voy al basurero a buscar, a sacar,**
> the night and there I go to the trashcan to look to get some
>
> you know? **No traía cigarros Camille, no traía Helen, no traía yo,**
> Camille didn't have any cigarettes, Helen didn't I didn't,
>
> **el Sr. de León** and I saw Dixie's bag crumpled up, so I figures she didn't
> Mr. Leon
>
> have any, **y ahí ando en los ceniceros buscando a ver dónde estaba**
> and there I'm going into the ashtrays looking to see where was
>
> **la . . .** I didn't care whose they were.
> the

It is easy to get the impression from listening to people do this that they do not really speak either language, and that they switch to one language because they are not sure how to say what they were starting to say in the other one. Actually, code-switchers can generally speak both languages without switching if need be: the woman in the preceding example will speak only Spanish with her relatives in Mexico and only English all day at work. In other cases, the speaker may be more comfortable in the local language than the dominant one but still be able to perform adequately enough in the dominant one to fulfill any task. In other words, code-switching is not a symptom of someone having never learned to truly speak a language: code-switchers always speak the local language perfectly, and as often as not, speak both languages fluently. One proof that code-switching is not a matter of deficiency is its rapidity and fluidity. If the switching were a matter of gaps in vocabulary or grammar, then we would expect pauses and "umms," but a quick listen to a Puerto Rican code-switching on a subway in New York will assure you that there is nothing of the kind.

Another sign that code-switching is not an impairment is that the switching is often not simply random but instead carefully keeps both languages separate according to particular traffic rules. For example, in code-switching between Spanish and English in the United States, one does not tack endings from one language onto words from another: one says neither *I was eat-iendo* yesterday for "I was eating" or *Ayer, mi hijo camina'ed to school* for "Yesterday, my son walked to school." There is also a rule that one does not switch in such a way that the sentence would be wrong in either language. This means that because English puts its adjectives before the noun, a Latino would not say *Hey, today I bought a car nuevo, y lo manejaba a la tienda. . . .* (". . . and I was driving it to the store . . ."), because you cannot say *a car new* in English. Instead, the person would likely say *Hey, today I bought a new car, y lo manejaba a la tienda . . .* , switching at a point that doesn't create a sentence that sounds like funny English. In the same way, the Chicana in the preceding example does not say *. . . and I saw Dixie's bolsa de papel arrugada* ("bag crumpled up"), because Spanish would require *la bolsa de papel de Dixie* "the bag of paper of Dixie." She switches at neutral points between whole clauses and sentences, so the traffic rules of both languages are left intact. In other countries, many code-switchers are less averse to using endings from one language on words from the other—as languages differ in sound interactions and sentence structures, code-switching rules vary from place to place. But most code-switchers are committed (subconsciously, of course) to keeping the languages separate on at least a broad level; no code-switchers simply gaggle along in a mad stew of the two languages (such as saying for "Yesterday I bought a new car," *Ayer I compré-d a car nuevo*).

Code-Switching in Other Climes

Code-switching is a response to a bicultural identity. Given how many bicultural identities imperialism has created worldwide, code-switching is a universal tendency, not just local to America's Latino immigrants, and not an exotic sort of thing popping up only in a few places. Code-switching can happen between any two languages if the conditions are right. Urban Senegalese code-switch between French and Wolof much as Latinos do here between English and Spanish. Here, the Senegalese language Wolof is in bold as Spanish was in the cigarette example:

C'est que **moom** féministe là   quoi **ta man** je défendais

it's   that   she   feminist   there you-know so me   I   defended

des idées **yoo**   **xamenta ni gemuma** ko sax.

   ideas   that you know   that I-not-believe it   even

"It's that she was a feminist while I defended ideas that I didn't even believe."

Meanwhile, educated people in the former SSRs of the Soviet Union often code-switch between Russian and Armenian, Russian and Kazakh, etc.; urban Kenyans code-switch between English and Swahili; you can walk around in Montreal and hear people switching like this between English and French. This is not a worldwide epidemic of deteriorating language abilities but simply the linguistic equivalent of the Indian shopkeeper wearing blue jeans and a turban. In the 1990s, the United States has received a great influx of Russian immigrants, and it is no surprise that many of them, feeling part American and part Russian, code-switch between English and Russian, thoroughly competent in both; Cantonese schoolchildren feeling Chinese with their parents and American at the mall, also code-switch, and it is so prevalent among Korean-Americans that they have a name for their switching, "Konglish."

Migrations of Words

Code-switchers are largely keeping the two languages involved separate, even though using them in the same conversations. However, when languages are in close contact like this, it is impossible that both will remain completely intact. Especially, once a local language encounters a dominant one, it will never be the same again; the question is only to what *extent* it will change. At the very least, it inevitably inherits massive amounts of vocabulary from the dominant language.

    We all know that some words in English are of foreign origin, like *pizza, ballet,* and *macho,* and if we learn another language we are particularly aware of how many of their words are taken from English, such as *super* and *pullover* in French. This, though, is only the very first hint of how vastly and deeply a language can drink of another one's vocabulary. When large numbers of speakers of a local language speak the dominant one as well, over time it is typical for even many basic, ordinary words in the local language to be joined, or just as often ousted, by equivalent ones from the dominant language.

English: A Bastard Vocabulary

For example, when Vikings invaded Great Britain in 787, they never took over the island but created enough trouble to be given the top half in 878, by which time English had taken a great many words from the Old Norse the Vikings spoke. It was the Vikings who replaced the *syle* we saw in the Old English Lord's Prayer with *give*. Also, before the Vikings, English had *shirts* and *ditches* but no *skirts* and *dikes; crafts* but no *skills;* one could *rise* but not *raise.*

Then in 1066, Great Britain was conquered by French speakers, who proceeded to run the country for two centuries. As typical conquerors, the French imposed their language upon the government and education, such that as odd as it seems to us today, for a long time the official language of England was French. English, then, became a local language as Wolof is today in Senegal, and like any local language, English first took in a number of words for things having to do with the la-di-da realms of life that the conquerors naturally dominated. Thus, words like *reign, pen, fashion, soldier,* and *cuisine* all came from French. French also gave us the words for meat, while the words for the living creatures themselves stayed English: *pig* is English, *pork* is French; *cow* is English, *beef* is French; *sheep* is English, *mutton* is French. But French didn't stop here; it even trickled into very ordinary parts of our vocabulary: *prayer, boot, stable, pain, porch, mountain, satisfy,* and *chair* and hundreds of other humble words all started out in French. Much of what makes Old English so opaque to us today is that it still had the now-lost original English equivalents to these words: a chair in Old English was a *setl.* Finally, English was then "invaded" in an abstract way by Latin, which became the common language of the educated in the 1500s and showered the language with another batch of new words like *anatomy, dictionary, multiply,* and *scene.*

These incursions of foreign vocabulary penetrated so deeply into the veins of English that today a mere 1 percent of its vocabulary is original English. But because these words are so basic to life—*father, sister, love, fight, and, but,* and a small but vital collection of four-letter words—they are 62 percent of the words most used. Yet all of these words are English to us; we are not showing off our command of foreign tongues to use words like *skill, boot,* or *multiply*—we are using English. Lots of languages' vocabularies have bastardy of this order in their histories: the Farsi that Iranians speak is half Arabic in its vocabulary; Farsi itself and Arabic have replaced over half of the original words in Turkish. The Chinese occupied Vietnam for one thousand years and predictably left their vocabulary over a third Chinese; Korean vocabulary is half Chinese.

To speakers of these languages, this is all buried in history, like the Old Norse, French, and Latin roots of most of our vocabulary. Yet when we see this happening before our eyes, we tend, in line with the idea that a language is something etched in stone rather than a living, evolving system, to see it as contamination. This brings us to the ambivalent relationship many people, Latino and non, have to what is called "Spanglish".

Spanglish: The Melting Pot in Action

The term *Spanglish* is a vague one with different meanings to different people; some people use it to refer to simple code-switching. For most people, however, Spanglish refers to the increasing tendency for first- and second-generation immigrants from Puerto Rico and Mexico to use a great many English words when speaking Spanish. Thus, many Chicanos say *brecas* for a car's brakes rather than the Spanish word *frenos; pushar* replaces *empujar, bica* replaces *bicicleta* for "bicycle." Often English idioms are translated word-for-word, creating expressions that a Spanish speaker with no contact with English would find incomprehensible. An example is *patearla* for "to kick it" in the sense of "relax," using the verb that means to literally kick, *patear,* plus *la* "it." A grandmother in Mexico who did not speak English would wonder what "it" the person was striking with their foot and what the purpose of such an activity might be.

This is the kind of Spanish we are most likely to hear young Latinos speaking; to hear them speaking a Spanish even close to devoid of English substitutions like this would be an exception, most typical of recent immigrants or children of parents who keep their children uniquely sheltered. Spanglish is nothing more or less than Spanish in America undergoing the same natural fertilization process that any language undergoes when spoken alongside another one long-term and when the dominant language's association with social and financial status exerts an irresistible pull. A speech variety serves partly for simple communication, but just as importantly to express an identity. Spanish with virtually no English words expresses the identity of, for example, the Mexicans who do not emigrate to the United States and spend their lives in a Spanish-speaking country living in Spanish, experiencing American culture only from a distance. This kind of Spanish, however, would not express the identity of the child of Mexican immigrants in the United States who goes to school in English, watches most of their television in English, has many English-speaking friends, and cannot imagine ever living in Mexico. The Spanish expressing this person's identity will incorporate English words just as English speakers surrounded by French incorporated French words into their vocabulary.

Our tendency, then, is to think of Spanglish as adulterated Spanish; even older Latinos and Spanish speakers who do not live in America tend to feel this way. Such feelings come from a sense that Spanglish speakers are straying from real Spanish. They are indeed straying from the standard dialect of Mexican Spanish. But the fact is that they could not do otherwise, and as we have seen, there is no reason that they shouldn't, because straying from standard Mexican Spanish is not a matter of decay but transformation. In other words, what Spanglish speakers are doing is creating a new dialect of Spanish just as English speakers created a new dialect of English while living under the sway of the French.

If the creation of a new kind of English during the French occupation of England was not a bastardization, then why is Spanglish one? There was a time when the originally French words like *aid* in English still "felt" as French to an English speaker as *cuisine* does to us now, and struck many as wrong in the same way as many Mexicans and Chicanos sense the use of *brecas* instead of *frenos* for "brakes" is wrong. There were those who urged English speakers to use the English equivalents—in the above cases, *help* and *cooking,* instead of French ones, to preserve the language. Yet today this is dusty history, and it is unclear to us what the big deal was about what we were losing. Would we really be somehow better off with *setl* than chair or *gelimplice* (which would by now have evolved into *limply*) instead of *suitable*? Imagine shopping for furniture looking for a *limply setl*—I don't know about you, but I'd much rather look for a suitable chair! In the same way, what is so anointed about *frenos* rather than *brecas*? Both convey their meaning. A thousand years from now, if Latinos preserve Spanish in this country, it will be—indeed could only be—in a form loaded with English vocabulary unknown in Mexico itself. This will be considered simply an alternative variety of Spanish in the same way as Canadian French is an alternative, but not invalid, variety of French.

Creoles: Hybrid Structure

We have seen that words are only the first layer of what speech is, and that dialects differ from a standard by degrees, ranging from mere words to accents and sentence structure. Along these lines, it is not surprising that languages change one another according to this same continuum.

Two Languages in the Same Mouths

For example, often, speakers of a language are bilingual in another language in such great numbers for such a long time that their language takes in not only words from the other one but even some structures, rather like people's pets are said to start looking like them after a while. Romanian is a typical case.

A language buff who learns some French, Spanish, Italian, and Portuguese senses them all as variations on one basic pattern. If you know one, then any of the other three come rather easily; French marches to the beat of its own drummer in some ways, especially its sound system, but Spanish and Portuguese are so similar that if you can read one you can pretty much read the other with minor adjustments, and even Spaniards and Italians can manage rough conversations. Romanian, however, is the queer one in the Romance crowd. Even with a solid command of the other four, a person who ventures Romanian continually gets tripped up by odd things foreign to the others.

For example, "the man" in French, Spanish, Italian, and Portuguese respectively is *l'homme, el hombre, l'uomo,* and *o homem.* Different languages, obviously, but their common heritage is clear—for one thing, all have "the man," with the definite article before the noun. In Romanian, however, it is *omul,* where *ul* is the equivalent of the definite article in the others. Why does Romanian place the definite article after the noun? Because of language contact. For centuries, many Romanian speakers were bilingual in Bulgarian or Albanian, and these languages place their definite articles after the noun— remember *dete to,* "child the," in Bulgarian on page 10 in the first chapter? Thus, besides taking vocabulary from other languages (Bulgarian and Albanian were two of five), Romanian gradually began "looking like" Bulgarian and Albanian in terms of this structural feature, a part of grammar. In the same way, in other Romance languages we learn that the masculine object pronoun serves as the generic one if we want to just say that something is done to an unspecified "it." In Spanish, if you say "I saw it" in reference to something inherently genderless like, say, the fall of Communism in Russia, you say *Lo ví.* In Romanian, though, the generic pronoun is the feminine one: *îl* is the equivalent of Spanish's masculine *lo,* but to say "I saw it" about the fall of Communism in Romania you would say *Am văzut-o,* "I have seen it," with the feminine pronoun. Why would Romanian have this little idiosyncrasy while its close Romance relatives don't? Contact with other languages again, in this case Albanian, which also handles its pronouns this way.

Creole Languages: One Language Out of Several

Language contact can transform a language even more, however. When it comes to words, a language can take on so many foreign ones that its vocabulary is virtually overhauled, and yet stay the same language. English, left with only 1 percent of its original vocabulary, is a case in point. English remains English because it did not take on the endings and structures of Old Norse, French, or Latin to any great extent, and it retained a key core of basic English words that get especially heavy use. But given the right conditions, a language can take on so much of another one's structure that the original structure no longer exists. In cases like these, the result is a new language entirely, roughly combining the structure of one with words from another. This is what a *creole* language is, and is how Haitian Creole, Jamaican patois, and Cape Verdeans' creole were born.

This kind of structural overhaul does not usually occur simply because of long-term bilingualism like the Romanian case. Instead of the language's original speakers transforming it in this way, it is generally non-native *learners* of the language who end up welding the structure from *their* language to the words from the one they are learning. As you might guess, this has generally taken place in unusual conditions, and it is no accident that creoles are mostly spoken by black or dark-skinned people from countries that were formerly plantation colonies run by Europeans.

Direct on the heels of the mid-millenium exploration of the New World we are taught about in school, England, France, Spain, Portugal, and Holland drew Africans from the western coast of Africa to work plantations and mines they set up in the various subtropical regions that had been "explored," especially the Caribbean and the coastal and inland regions nearby. There are dozens of languages spoken on Africa's western coast, and slaves on a given plantation usually came from various areas and thus had no one language in common. In terms of practicality and the eternal power factor, the language of the masters was the choice as the language for communication. This was especially true for children born on the plantations, who never knew a setting where an African language was "the language"; that is, the only one spoken around them as they acquired the power of speech.

However, working from sunrise to sundown in a field is not the best setting for learning a new language. Comunication between masters and slaves was minimal, and as a result, slaves largely learned words without learning the grammar to put them together with. Yet the need for a way to communicate remained, and thus what slaves did was use these words within the grammars they already had, their native ones. Often, the slaves spoke languages that were related in the same way that the Romance languages were, so that if each used the European words with their particular native grammar, the result was comprehensible to most of the other slaves. Using this combination of European words and African structures on a day-to-day basis over decades, slaves on a plantation gradually crystallized it into a speech variety able to communicate observations, requests, desires, commands, and after a while poetry, songs, jokes—in other words, it became a language in its own right. This is what a creole language is.

Creole is often thought to refer to the language of descendants of slaves in Louisiana. Indeed, a creole language emerged in the way I described on plantations in Louisiana, using French words with African structures. However, this process occurred in colonies run by all of the big five powers, such

that there are also creoles with English words (such as Gullah of South Carolina, Jamaican patois, and Sranan of Suriname), Spanish (such as Papiamentu
of Curaçao), Dutch (such as the now extinct Negerhollands of St. Thomas, a
Virgin Island), and other French ones (such as Haitian and Martiniquan). Despite their scarcity on lists of official languages, creoles are the home languages
of nations in the Caribbean and many other places, including Mauritius,
Cape Verde, Guinea-Bissau, Guyana, and French Guiana. A Haitian politician
speaks to the media in French or English but speaks Haitian Creole at home
and with friends. A black person living on one of the Sea Islands off the coast
of South Carolina, depicted in Gloria Naylor's novel *Mama Day* and the
film *Daughters of the Dust*, will speak English to us but Gullah Creole as their
colloquial variety.

Haitian Creole demonstrates how creoles combine European words
with African sentence structures. African sentence structures are quite different from anything we are used to in languages like Spanish, German, or Russian. For example, where we use a preposition *to* in a sentence like *Koku gave
the crab to her*, the language Fon of Togo and Benin will use two verbs strung
together without any preposition:

Koku so ason o na e.
Koku take crab the give her

Thus, where we say *bring to*, Fon expresses the "*to*-ness" by using the verb *give*.
Fon also (like Romanian, Bulgarian, and Albanian) puts *the* after nouns: *ason
o* "crab the."

Because many of the slaves brought to Haiti spoke Fon and closely related languages with the same sentence structures, Haitian uses French words,
but in sentence structures that are part of what makes the language incomprehensible to a French speaker. "He brought the book to his father" is *Il a
amené le livre à son père* in French, but in Haitian it is:

Li pran liv-la   ba papa-li.
he take book-the give father-his

(*Ba* comes from an archaic French verb "to give," *bailler*.)

Note also that Haitian also has "book-the" and "father-his" like Fon has
"crab-the." These are only a couple of ways in which Haitian combines Fon
grammar with French words.

Of course if it were that simple, then this would be a kind of Fon where
the vocabulary had been overhauled the way English's was. However, Fon
grammar is only partly reproduced. There is also a fair amount of French
grammar, some grammar traceable to strategies that all people use when having learned a new language incompletely, and some grammar that Haitian has

just created on its own. This means that not only a French person has to learn Haitian as a separate language, but even a Fon speaker would. In other words, Haitian is a brand new language.

"Oh, It's Just a Little English, a Little Portuguese, a Little African . . ."

The temptation is extremely great, nevertheless, to think of creoles as not real languages. Even their speakers are often of this sentiment; Jamaican patois, for example, is regarded as a scourge by most educated Jamaicans exactly as Black English is regarded here as a broken down English of which school-children must be cured. This is partly because creoles tend to have done away with the endings in the European language that provided their words: "he runs" in Jamaican patois is *im ron*, "he walked" is *im en waak*, using the separate word *en* (which started as *been*) instead of the ending *-ed*. We English speakers know how hard it is to learn to use the long lists of verbal endings in languages like Spanish (*hablo, hablas, habla, hablamos, habláis, hablan*). It's hard enough to learn these endings when they are taught carefully on a black-board; imagine instead having to just pick them up from listening to them being used orally at high speed. African slaves were in a situation where they didn't even get to converse at any length with Europeans, and naturally ended up having to do without things like these endings. Thus, there are no creoles with long lists of endings for a number of different tenses with endings different for each of three classes of verb.

These endings are part of what we perceive as making a language complex, but in fact, endings are but one of many things that make a language complex, and many languages around the world have no endings. Mandarin Chinese, for example, has none, and yet we are all aware that learning Chinese is much harder for an English speaker than learning French or Spanish.

Creoles, too, despite their lack of endings, have their quirky aspects that challenge the learner. In Haitian, to say *Bouki is my father,* you say:

Bouki papa-m.
Bouki father-my

So this is just one of those languages with no *to be* like Russian, right? Not so simple, actually. If you say *Bouki is a doctor,* then you say:

Bouki se yon doktè.
Bouki is a   doctor

Why the difference? Because in Haitian, you only use "to be" when what is "be'd" has an article *a* or *the.* So English is simpler compared to Haitian here, because we use "to be" whether there is an article or not.

Now, how do you say *Bouki is under the table?* If "under the table" is *anba tab-la,* then it should be:

Bouki se anba tab-la
Bouki   is under table-the

Right? After all, it's *the* table. Actually, though, you don't use a "to be" here either; it's:

Bouki anba tab-la.
Bouki under table-the

This is because you don't use *to be* in Haitian at all when you are talking about *where* someone or something is in a simple sentence like this one. This is something that takes practice, just like learning that German often its verbs on the end of the sentence sticks.

But then, how would you ask "Where is he?", if "where" is *kotè* and "he" is *li?* Well, if you don't use *to be* when talking about where someone or something is, how about:

Kotè li?
where he

Actually, usually not—even if you are talking about location, you usually have to use a "to be" if you ask a question. So how about:

Kotè se li?
where is he

Well, still no. In questions, *to be* has to go at the end. Well, then, what else could it be but this?

Kotè li se?
where he is

Close but no cigar. Actually, it's:

Kotè li ye?
where he is

What's this *ye?* Well, because there is this concern with location, *ye* must be a special "to be" used when talking about location, but then only when it comes at the end of a sentence.

That's odd enough, but still wrong! Here is "Who is he?" which has nothing to do with where the "he" in question is:

Kimoun li ye?
who   he is

Actually, *ye* is the *to be* you use whenever *to be* comes at the end of a sentence, whether you are talking about location or anything else—seafood, pets, hair. Thus there are two verbs *to be.* You only use *se* in statements, and then only when the predicate has an article, and then only as long as you are talking about what someone or something is. If you ask a *question* involving being, you use not *se* but *ye,* and *ye* comes not between the question word and the subject as in English or French (*Où est-il?* "Where is he?"), but at the end of the sentence.

But *ye* isn't simply the "*to be* for questions", because you also use it when *to be* comes at the end of a sentence that *isn't* a question:

Li vwe kotè ou ye.
he sees   where you are

"He sees where you are."

Obviously, this is no "baby talk" French. A French person could "make up" Haitian neither by simply speaking French with no *to be* nor by simply using *c'est,* the source of *se,* everywhere. They have to learn a whole new way of using *to be,* including the fact that there are two different "to be"s. All creoles are full of things like this.

Of course, another reason creoles often seem like "not really languages" is because they are only spoken, rarely written down or used in formal situations. There is some poetry written in creoles, such as the Jamaican poetry of Louise Bennett; the Bible has been translated into many creoles; there is the occasional novel; and there are even Papiamentu newspapers. But overall, it is the European languages that have official status in creole-speaking countries. English is the language of education in Jamaica, French is the language of Haitian newspapers, Portuguese is what a Cape Verdean must learn for upward mobility or contact with the outside world. Thus, like Appalachian English, Black English, Cockney English, or Brooklynese, creoles are generally perceived as kitchen-sink, six-pack affairs by speakers and observers alike. They are often cherished as jolly bad habits on the local level, but considered a bit of an embarrassment on the public level, like dear old drunk Uncle Sid—you would prefer to keep him home, but if you have to take him to the cotillion you cover him up with stiff, itchy clothes and just hope you can keep him quiet enough through the evening to keep up appearances.

Yet in fact, creole languages are further demonstrations of what we have already seen, that there is no such thing as fluent human speech that is bad grammar. Faced with finding a way to communicate where no one African language was spoken by everybody and where whites weren't around enough to pass on their language, African slaves did not simply cobble together a bit of this and a bit of that into a make-do contraption of a language and settle down into centuries of making do with bad grammar. Humans must have fluent, coherent, nuanced speech, and accordingly, what they created were brand new *languages*. The results of this experiment came out the same way every time. The English also colonized Australia and the islands to the north and eastward, and the Aborigines and Melanesians they roped into their employ created creoles as well. One way those speakers of 800 languages in Papua New Guinea communicate today is with an English creole called Tok Pisin, for example. There are Spanish creoles spoken in the Philippines, there is a creole Malay spoken by people of Chinese ancestry in Malaysia, a creole Arabic spoken in Uganda and Kenya by black descendants of soldiers displaced from Sudan a century ago, and creoles based on languages none of us have even heard of spoken in places we will never visit. The grammars of all these creoles have had to be worked out carefully in thick, obscure grammars only a linguist could love. In other words, they're languages.

From Improvisation to a Whole New Tune: An Unbroken Path

Thus, languages transform one another along the same continuum that dialects differ from standards along, from mere words through to sentence structure. Whether sprinkled with new words or grammatically overhauled, the result is never "neither fish nor fowl" nor bad grammar, but simply a new variation on the original. Just as dialects can fall at any point along a continuum of difference from a standard, a speech variety can fall at any point along a continuum of depth of language contact.

Black English, for example, falls at the same point in relation to standard English as Romanian falls in relation to typical Romance. Just as Romanian has a few structural features adapted from Bulgarian, Albanian, and nearby languages, Black English has a few features adapted from the African languages slaves in the South spoke. There have been claims, such as during the Oakland Ebonics controversy of 1997, that Black English is an African language with English words, in other words, a creole English like Haitian is a creole French. It is obvious, however, that Black English does not contain any African sentence structures as foreign to us as the stringing of verbs together or the placement of articles after the noun, and that in general, it is a kind of English. The depiction of Black English as an African language arises partly out of an understandable desire to legitimize the dialect, but has the problem of stipulating that if Rocky Balboa says *Ain't it nice, you an' me heah tugeddah?*, then it's English, but that if a black person says *Ain't it nice, you an' me heah tugethah?* it's African.

That awkwardness simply shows that because language contact is a continuum, African influence operates in degrees. While Haitian is too deeply transformed by African languages to be considered a kind of French, Black English was influenced by African languages, but only once over lightly. While in places like Haiti, slaves often worked in gangs as large as 500, most plantations in the American South were much smaller, many of them properly small farms. This lent most American slaves more contact with English speakers, and this was reinforced by the fact that they often worked side-by-side with indentured white servants from Great Britain and Ireland. As a matter of fact, most of the things differentiating Black English from standard English came from these servants' colloquial dialects, including the "regularity" *be*; African languages largely contributed features of accent.

Creoles in the United States

Some slaves in America did work in conditions that led to creoles, and one other formed in a different kind of situation.

Gullah

In the Sea Islands off the coast of South Carolina and a bit inland, slaves grew rice, which not only required massive manpower but thrived best in marshy terrain where whites could not work because they lacked blacks' inherited immunity to malaria. Here, blacks worked in conditions similar to Caribbean plantation societies—in large numbers with few whites around—and the result was a creole, Gullah. Because many of the first slaves brought to South Carolina had already worked in Barbados, Gullah is in large part a continuation of the West Indian patois spoken in Barbados and in Jamaica, Belize, Antigua, and other nations. Gullah speakers can converse fairly well in their language with people speaking Jamaican patois, for example. As such, Gullah is a flavor of West Indian patois spoken right here in America.

The Gershwin brothers' opera *Porgy and Bess* was derived from a play *Porgy*, whose authors Dubose and Dorothy Heyward were Charleston, South Carolina residents with a long-standing interest in the folkways of Gullah-speaking blacks. The characters in *Porgy*, set in backwater quarters in Charleston, would have spoken Gullah in real life, and the original play was written in a dialogue inflected with Gullahisms to connote the flavor of their speech. Virginia Geraty has translated the play into Gullah itself, and here is a sample:

Bess: Uh tell you de trut'! Porgy me man now!

Crown: Uh yent hab uh laugh since two, tree week!

Bess: 'E fuh true, Crown. Uh de onlies' 'ooman Porgy ebbuh hab. Ef uh yent gone home tuh Porgy, 'e gwi' stan' same lukkuh (*he is going to be just like a*) little chile wuh loss 'e Ma!

Crown: Wuh uh wan' wid odduh 'ooman? Uh hab 'ooman! Dat 'ooman duh (*is*) you!

Gullah is not as far from standard English as Haitian is from French, but because of the accent as well as some unusual features like the *to be* form *duh,* and the word for plural "you," *hunnuh,* it can be virtually impossible for standard speakers to understand when the creole is spoken at regular speed, similar to the effect with Scots English.

In the 1600s, when Florida was still a Spanish possession, slaves in Georgia would often escape to the Florida interior, often intermarrying with Native American ex-slaves also taking refuge there. The Native Americans came from many tribes and were called collectively Seminoles, a distortion of the Spanish word *cimarrón* for "runaway." Some of the biracial progeny of these unions relocated to Oklahoma when the United States annexed Florida in 1819, and some of these were settled in the small town of Bracketville, Texas in return for helping whites fight Indians there (an ironic story depicted in the television movie *Buffalo Soldiers*). Their descendants were found recently to still speak Gullah, and thus this variety of West Indian patois has been passed down for a century and a half in a state where one would think English and Spanish had long eradicated all other forms of speech.

Louisiana Creole French

Meanwhile, when Louisiana was still a French territory in the 1700s, slaves were imported to work on plantations there, and they developed a French creole, sometimes called Gombo, still spoken by many blacks there today, especially poor, isolated rural ones (the characters in the film *Eve's Bayou* speak some phrases in it). It was once also spoken as far east as Alabama. After Haiti became independent in 1804, many planters fled with their slaves to Louisiana, and partly for that reason, Louisiana Creole is similar to Haitian, and thus just as Gullah is a variety of West Indian patois on our soil, Louisiana Creole can be thought of as a variant of Caribbean French creole spoken natively here. Here is someone describing how Africans used to make drums:

Ye te   konnen pran en bari, avek en but lapo,
they PAST know   take a   barrel with a   piece skin

e ye te   gen shofe lapo pu li vini stiff.
and they PAST have heat   skin for it come stiff

Mo pans se de zafe   ye mennen isi dan slavery.
I   think it   things they bring   here in   slavery

"They used to take a barrel with a piece of skin, and they used to heat the skin until it became stiff. I think these are things that were brought over here with slavery."

What makes this a creole is features like the decidedly un-French use of *konnen* "to know" (from French *connaître*) to mean "used to," and the use of particles like *te* to express the past instead of endings.

Louisiana Creole has developed in a symbiotic relationship with the Cajun French spoken by poor whites. Cajun is not a creole, but a dialect of Canadian French, brought to the region by immigrants from Nova Scotia when the British took over Canada in the mid-1700s. (The Nova Scotia region was called Acadia; *Cajun* is a vernacular form of *Acadian*.) Thus, Cajun is a transplanted variety of the Canadian French still spoken by the Montrealers and Ottawans who stayed in Canada, which we saw a sample of on page 5 in the first chapter. Here is a sample of Cajun:

Eux-autes serait   contents—tu   les   appelles 'oir,
they   would be happy   you them call   see

parce que ça   travaille tard . . . ils travaillont tard,
because   they work   late   they work   late

so tu peux les appeler 'oir équand tu pourrais les prendre.
so you can   them call   see when   you could   them take

"They'd be happy—you call them and see, because they work late . . . they work late, so you can call them and see when you could catch them."

This is basically French, with endings, direct and indirect object pronouns like *les* placed before the verb, etc. A French person can make it out after some adjustment. However, it differs from standard French in many ways. *Eux-autes*, from *eux-autres* "them-others," is built on the same plan as the standard Spanish *nosotros* and *vosotros*, which began as "we others" and "you others"; indeed Cajun also has *nous-autes* for "we" and *vous-autes* for plural "you". (This is another demonstration of how arbitrary the notion of standard is: *nous-autes* is considered "vulgar" French but *nosotros*, originally "we-others," is high Spanish!) The use of *ça* "that" for "they" and the ending -*ont* instead of -*ent* in the third person plural (*travaillont*) are other differences from standard French.

Cajun and the creole have been influencing one another for centuries just as white and black Southern English have. Who knew that Canadian

French and a cousin of Haitian Creole had been miscegenating for centuries in a state within this supposedly English-only nation? Yet we see the results of this mating dance in the lyrics to Zydeco music.

The situation is further enriched by the fact that European French spoken by descendants of the French colonists themselves continued to be spoken in Louisiana well into the twentieth century. This had the result that today there is a variety in between French and the creole, which has as many French features as creole ones and is thus not quite classifiable as either one. Within this little state, then, French, the intermediate variety, and the creole have been a kind of living demonstration of how language contact operates in degrees. Note also that the Louisiana Creole passage has the English words *stiff* and *slavery* in it, which we would expect because English plays such a large part in all Louisianans' lives just as it does in Spanglish speakers'.

Sadly, however, Louisiana Creole is not simply changing, but gradually disappearing in favor of English. There are no longer any people who speak only, or mainly, creole, which is usually a sign that a language is on its way to extinction. When it dies, however, a fascinating language hybrid will have graced our country for three centuries.

Hawaiian "Pidgin"

A third and last creole spoken in the United States is Hawaiian "Pidgin." By the late 1800s, when the United States began taking over Hawaii to put its fertile soil to use in plantation agriculture, slavery was no longer legal. Thus, Chinese immigrants were imported to work the plantations on what was nominally a temporary contract arrangement, but that as often as not became a lifetime of unofficial slavery. Many Chinese also immigrated to California, and when interethnic tensions there led to a ban on further Chinese immigration in 1882, they were replaced by Japanese immigrants. Similar mainland tensions led the Japanese to be banned in 1908 in favor of Filipinos, as well as small numbers of Koreans and Puerto Ricans, and all of this time the plantation foremen had been Portuguese. Here was a situation as ripe for the development of a creole as Caribbean plantations had been two centuries before.

Adults were soon communicating in a rudimentary but functional pidgin, pidgins being precursors to more fully developed creoles. It was the immigrants' children in schools who transformed the pidgin into a true language—that is, a creole—around 1900. The language is still called "pidgin" in popular parlance, and remains the colloquial speech of Hawaiians of all ethnicities, used most and in the form furthest from English by people with the least education. Like Black English, Hawaiian pidgin is popularly regarded as bad English when in fact it is simply different English, with its own structures and quirks, as well as a notoriously colorful vocabulary with words from Hawaiian itself as well as the various languages spoken by the immigrants who came to Hawaii over a century ago: *ono* "delicious" is Hawaiian, *skoshi* for "a little" is from Japanese *sukoshi,* etc. Here is a passage in Pidgin from the wonderful pop "dictionary" of Hawaiian "Pidgin," *Pidgin to da Max:*

> Who wen cockaroach da orange juice from da icebox aftah I wen kapu am? I gon kill da buggah!

Wen is the marker of past, having started as *been. Kapu* means to make forbidden. Perhaps the feature of Hawaii's Pidgin that stands out most to speakers and non-speakers alike is the use of *stay* as an equivalent to standard English *-ing: Dey stay run* means "they are running" or that they run on a regular basis.

Just as the writing of the standard obscures the fact that each language comes in many varieties equal in the eyes of God, the Rand McNally perspective obscures that languages also constantly bleed into one another to varying degrees, like the ingredients of a stew. French left thousands of words in English, and later in many places, African and Oceanic languages left their very sentence structures in English creating new languages entirely. Spanish originated in Spain but is bathed in Arabic words; in South America Indian languages have added vocabulary and some sentence patterns to Spanish; in Curaçao, Colombia, and the Philippines there are Spanish creoles; in Ecuador there is even a special Spanish-Quechua hybrid with Spanish words and Quechua endings. Portuguese comes in its continental variety, in a variety spoken in Brazil that is partly creolized in some regions, in creoles spoken on the west coast of Africa like Cape Verdean, and in other creoles spoken on the coast of India, where missionary and commercial activity introduced words and structures from languages like Marathi and Tamil into the language. Most speakers of Swahili actually speak creole or partly creolized versions of Swahili.

And the wonder is that in every case, what people are speaking is a full language that would be a challenge for the foreigner to learn. Languages change, to various extents, in various directions; languages mix, to various extents, in various directions. Changing and mixing are as inherent to the life of a language as they are to the lives of the humans who speak them, but despite the upheaval, human speech always "resolves to the tonic chord," to speak musically, remaining always a coherent system. Thus, dialects of a language emerge within a context of constant transformation and cross-fertilization that nevertheless always maintains fundamental stability, just as the inexorable operations of evolution have produced an endless array of viable creatures without developing "misfires" reverting in shame to sucking ooze on the bottom of the sea. Colloquial dialects and mixed speech varieties don't suck ooze—they are evidence of the life force.

Exercises

1. These are some simple sentences in Haitian Creole. The words are from French but the sound patterns and sentence structures are so different that the result is a new language entirely. Have the students try to converse in Haitian, using English words as well to keep things going.

Bonjou	Hello	*Sa y'ap fe?*	What are you doing?
Mèsi	Thank you	*Ou konprann?*	Do you understand?
M'kontan wè ou.	I am happy to see you.	*Mwen vle manje.*	I want to eat.
Kouman ou ye?	How are you?	*Mwen pa te konn sa.*	I didn't know that.
Orevwa.	Goodbye	*Tande'm!*	Listen to me!
Kouman ou rele?	What is your name?	*Li yon bèl fanm.*	She's a pretty woman.
Mwen rele . . .	My name is . . .	*M'ap chante.*	I am singing.
Moun ki kote ou ye?	Where are you from?	*Ou toujou fatige.*	You are always tired.
M'prale.	I'm leaving.	*Pare!*	Get ready!
Ban'm repo'm!	Leave me alone!	*Kotè li ye?*	Where is he?

Here are some pronunciation tips:

- *Ou* is pronounced *oo*.

- An *n* after a vowel makes the vowel nasal, like the French *bon*, which is pronounced not "Bonn" but "bawng"; thus *mwen* is "mweng". There is no need to worry too much about this, though.

- There are no "silent e's"; therefore *fatige* is pronounced "fah-tee-GEH".

2. Have your students look up where each of these English words originally came from:

vodka	Russian	*cruise*	Dutch	*molasses*	Portuguese
giraffe	Italian	*sauna*	Finnish	*curry*	Tamil
tea	Chinese	*thug*	Hindi	*polo*	Tibetan
sputnik	Russian	*zero*	Arabic	*parka*	Russian
typhoon	Chinese	*coffee*	Turkish	*sherbet*	Arabic
jungle	Hindi	*gung-ho*	Chinese	*shampoo*	Hindi
boondocks	Tagalog	*punch*	Hindi	*knapsack*	Dutch

3. Are there any student groups in your class who code-switch between English and another language after hours? If so, have them write down a conversation they might have in which they code-switch, translating the foreign language passages. Have them see if there are any particular reasons for why they switch at the points they do.

4

The Linguistic Rain Forest

When the world was still in black and white and they hadn't invented cholesterol, there were a number of books written for the general public about "the languages of the world." They were good reading, but they reflected their times in a tacit assumption that "the world" was basically Europe and some other places. Books like this tended to give long, loving attention to the Romance and Germanic languages, respectful coverage of Slavic and some other European languages, and then only nod politely at languages spoken elsewhere.

Although ethnocentrism surely played some part in this, the approach also made a certain sense, in that in those days languages like French, Spanish, German, and Swedish were the ones Americans were most likely to encounter in the United States. The multicolored ethnic terrain we are familiar with in today's America did not exist until the Immigration Act of 1965 loosened decades of restrictions designed to keep the numbers of non-white immigrants as low as possible. As such, the America of *I Love Lucy* was one where the typical white person could go through life without ever meeting a Filipino, African, or Pacific Islander, and might encounter an Asian only on a trip to a Chinatown or as an occasional servant. This was not only because America was a segregated country, but because people of these extractions simply were not present here in the large numbers we now take for granted.

Those times are now gone and virtually unrecognizable to us, and what this means is that the foreign languages we are most likely to encounter in our lives are no longer the grand old standards like French and German. On the contrary, when we hear that eighty languages are spoken by schoolchildren in Oakland, California, French and German are mere static compared to the

61

languages that now occupy center stage: Russian, Amharic, Vietnamese, Cantonese, Hindi—what popular linguists back in those days thought of as "the other languages."

As it happens, because these languages are mostly unrelated to the schoolroom staples (like Spanish) that we most often learn, they are often built in ways we would never imagine a language could be. It is easy to get an impression in America that in any language, the subject comes first and is followed by a verb, that things like plurality and tense are expressed with endings, that in a sentence like *I broke the window*, *I* will be the subject and *window* will be the object no matter what language you are speaking, and that most other languages seem to have more prefixes and endings to memorize than English but that basically, speaking another language means learning a new set of words and getting the hang of a few variations on our way of expressing things, like saying *Yo lo tengo* "I it have" in Spanish instead of "I have it."

This chapter will take us on a trip through eight languages spoken by large immigrant groups in the United States today, which children in classrooms now commonly speak as home languages. Good old French, Spanish, and German are marvelous in their ways, but in relation to English, they are essentially business as usual. The variety of words and grammars from Africa, Asia, and beyond surrounding us in today's America is literally dazzling.

Russian

Especially since the fall of communism in Russia in 1991, Russians have been immigrating to the United States in ever larger numbers. Once mostly encountered here as visitors or defectors, Russians have now become an American ethnic group large enough that if the Russian immigrant moves to the right city, they can manage to live in Russian without ever learning more than functional English. Russian-speaking children are now common in many schools; in large classes at Berkeley I can count on having at least two or three Russian students; walking down the street in some cities one is as likely to catch Russian being spoken as Spanish.

Russians' language belongs to the same Indo-European group that the Romance and Germanic languages do, and in broad outline feels to us like "family" if we learn it. It is also, however, one of the most complex languages on earth, and often leaves the foreign learner wondering how anyone could speak it without intense concentration.

Like Latin, Russian declines its nouns; that is, a noun takes a different ending depending on how it is used in a sentence. In Russian, *bus* by itself is *avtobus*. However, if you want to talk about the color (*tsvyet*) of the bus, you need an ending: the *tsvjet avtobus-**a***. If you turn your back to the bus you turn it to the *avtobus-**u***. If you are in the bus you are in the *avtobus-ye*, but you block traffic with the *avtobus-**om***.

So far this is no big deal, especially if one has had any Latin. But for one thing, Russian has more declensions than Latin, which has no equivalent of the *-om* ending. Besides this, Russian endings have a way of "bleeding" back into the noun and creating any number of subrules and outright exceptions. For example, some words have a quiet little hint of a "y" sound on the end, which an English speaker barely perceives. In Roman letters, this sound is indicated with an apostrophe (just like the glottal stop in Ojibwe; the apostrophe tends to be used as a kind of "et al." sign for little sounds that we and Western Europeans process as odd). *Stil'* for "style" is one of these, pronounced "steel," but then with a slight tightening of the tongue at the end. This little hint of a "y" sound seems like it must be a trivial little part of accent that we don't need to really bother with if we don't feel like it. But you do end up having to think about it, because it tends to mess up the basic noun endings we just saw. Sometimes it does this in a way that makes sense to us: you turn your back to the *avtobus-**u***, but if you refused to tear your sweatshirt in 1983, you turned your back to *stil-**yu***—here, the *-u* ending just picked up the "y." But other times, the little sound screws up the ending in a way you just have to know. Block traffic with the *avtobus-**om**,* but show that you're "all that" with *stil . . . -**yom***, right? No, for some reason it's *stil-**yem***.

If you're talking about something living, then if it is the object of the sentence it takes the possessive ending. Just as the color of the bus is the color of the *avtobus-**a**,* the color of the man is the color of the *chelovyek-**a***. If you see the bus you just see the *avtobus*—no ending— but if you see the man you see the *chelovyek-**a***—seeing "of him," so to speak. And on top of all this, this is just masculine nouns—there are different endings for the feminine and neuter ones plus a special plural set.

The other marvelous thing about Russian is that its verbs change according to whether the action is done over a period of time or in one shot. In French or Spanish, we learn to distinguish the imperfect from the pretertite (in French the *passé simple*) along these lines: "The students were learning their lessons when the bell rang" in French is *Les étudiants apprenaient leurs leçons quand la cloche a sonné;* and in Spanish is *Los estudiantes aprendían sus lecciones cuando sonó la campana.* In both cases, the imperfect is used for the ongoing action of studying, and the *passé simple* or preterite is used for the immediate and one-time occurrence of the bell ringing. In Russian, one must think about this "one-shot" versus "ongoing" distinction not only in the past, but at all times.

What makes this particularly tricky in Russian is that attending to this distinction is nothing as simple as mastering a set of endings. For example, if someone asks you what you are doing while you are writing a letter, you say *Ja pishu* "I am writing." But if somebody tells you to write a letter, then they tell you not just *Pishi!* but **Napishi!** The *na-* makes this one-shot instead of ongoing, and just *Pishi!* would be incorrect. That alone doesn't look so hard, but the problem is that making the verb one-shot is not just a matter of tacking on *na-*: there are all kinds of ways to do it, and you never know which one a verb is going to use. If you spent the night drinking beer, then you *pil,* but if you chugged down a glass of beer in thirty seconds, you did not *na-pil,* you **vypil** (with *y* being that "llllll" sound that Lucy Ricardo used to make when she was in trouble, mentioned in Chapter Two). Which prefix you choose is not based on anything like sounds, the way you know a Spanish verb takes certain endings if it ends in *-ar* (*hablar* "to speak") and others if it ends in *-er* (*comer* "to eat"). You just have to know.

And then you can't even be sure that the difference is going to be a matter of a prefix. As often as not, it is expressed with a suffix. If you began to see the light over time, then you *nachinal* to see it, but if you began making a meal at 4:00 P.M., then you *nachal* making it. Notice also that in this case, the one-shot ending is shorter and basic (*nachal*), and the ongoing one has the add-on (*nachinal*), instead of the other way around like the "one-shot" *vypil* being the one that has the add-on. Again, you never know which suffix it might be. If you got so hot that you ran over and opened a window with a gasp, then you *otkryl* it, but if you talk about having opened the window every day at 8:00 A.M., you say that you *otkryval* it.

But we're not done yet. Often it is not a matter of tacking something on either end but just changing a vowel. If a bird flew into your yard daily to feed at the feeder, it *priljetala* (*-a* is the feminine ending because the word for "bird" *ptitsa* is feminine), but if it flew in once and never came back, then it *priljetela.*

And finally, sometimes you have to use two different verbs altogether. If a Russian teaches you that *poidjom* means "let's go," you naturally think that *poid-* is the word for *go.* Yet if a few minutes later someone asks you what you do on Sundays, to say "We go to the movies" you say *My* **khodim** *v kino,* not *My poidjom v kino.* And, of course, all of these verbs have their irregularities just as the ones in French and German do.

Yet despite all this, Russian children are rattling along happily in this language by the age of six, doing all of this without a second thought. Talk to many Russians, and they will tell you they never actually thought about how complicated it all is: "*Pishu, na-pishu, poidjom, khodim*—yeah, I say *na-pishu* when I'm doing it just once . . . I guess that *is* kind of weird. . . ."

Chinese

We often hear that there are a number of Chinese dialects such as Mandarin, Cantonese, and Taiwanese. These are dialects in name only, however, because in reality they are distinct languages, as different from one another as the Romance languages. They are called dialects because they are all written with the same Chinese characters, and are united within one nation with a strong sense of its history and uniqueness. Yet a Cantonese speaker has to learn Mandarin as a new language and vice versa, and a movie in Mandarin needs subtitles to be shown to a Cantonese-speaking audience. We can intuit the difference from seeing this sentence in both:

Mandarin:	Wŏ	bèi	rén	tōu le	chēzi.
Cantonese:	Ngóh	béi	yàhn	tāu-jó	ga chē.
	I	by	person	stolen	car

"I've had my car stolen."

Chinese is often described based on the Mandarin dialect because this is the one used as the national standard in China. However, most of the Chinese immigrants who came to the United States starting in the mid-1800s to found the Chinese-American communities of today were Cantonese speakers. Many Mandarin speakers have come since the Immigration Act of 1965, as well as speakers of another dialect, Taiwanese, but the Chinese we hear walking through a Chinatown is usually Cantonese.

Chinese varieties have none of the noun declensions that Russian does, nor do Chinese speakers use different verb forms depending on whether an action is abrupt or continuous, or depending on anything, for that matter. Chinese varieties have no endings at all, as you can see in the preceding examples. Yet these languages are as difficult for us to get a real hang of as Russian.

In English, the meaning of a syllable changes according to its sounds: what makes *pat* and *bat* mean different things is the different first letters. In Cantonese, this is true as well. But in addition, a syllable's meaning also changes completely depending on which of six tones you utter it on, some flat, others swooping up or down to various extents. Thus, the word *fan* can mean "divide," "powder," "advise," "grave," "excited," or "share" depending just on its tone. (Mandarin is the "easy" dialect, with only four tones!) Needless to say, the possibilities for bizarre misunderstandings are legion for foreigners who have not mastered the tones, especially in cases like the Mandarin syllable *ma*, which among other things can mean either *mother* or *horse!*

The Chinese writing system consists not of an alphabet but of pictures, called *characters,* of each concept. Needless to say, this exerts more of a load on the memory than a mere alphabet, and one needs to know thousands of characters to even read a newspaper (and therefore the Chinese man you see on the bus reading one has this many in his head and doesn't give it a second thought). It's quite a task but has its short cuts. For one, *combinations* of characters are as important as individual ones. Most of the time, the several things that a syllable can mean depending on its tone are all written with the character for one of the six meanings, combined with another sign telling you which of the meanings is intended. For example, this is the sign for horse: 马. Combining this with the sign for woman 女 signifies "the *ma* that is a woman," that is, "mother": 妈. Combining the horse sign with the one for mouth 口 (actually two of them) means "the *ma* that involves chattering," that is, "scold": 骂. And so on. The characters we see on signs in Chinatowns and on menus in Chinese restaurants can look like dense, involved scrawls to us, but usually what looks so busy is just a combination of two or three basic signs.

Yet this is definitely a much harder writing system to learn to read and produce than are our twenty-six letters, even with their irregularities. The very process of learning to read well enough to make out a popular magazine article occupies all of a Chinese child's basic education, whereas for English speakers, the basic decoding process is learned before the end of elementary school.

Vietnamese

Vietnamese is a language like the Chinese ones where meaning depends on the syllables' tones. Like Cantonese, it has six different tones, such that the syllable *ma* can mean "cheek," "ghost," "rice shoot," "tomb," "but," or, yes, "horse"—again, depending on the tone. (As mentioned in the last chapter, Vietnamese's vocabulary is more than a third Chinese, which is why their *ma* can mean "horse," like Chinese's.) Each of these tones is indicated with a special mark on the vowels. These little hooks and crooks in written Vietnamese make it look randomly sprinkled to us:

Tôi sẽ trả lời cho người đó trước.

I   will pay word give person that before

"I will answer that person first."

Other of these little squiggles and baubles allow the Vietnamese to reflect the actual variety of their vowel sounds in a way that English does not. For example, the sounds that *u* stands for in *duty* and *but* are hardly the same. In Vietnamese, *u* is used for the *duty* "u," while *â* is used for the *but* sound.

If you look closely at that preceding sentence and how the words are ordered, it might remind you of some other languages we have seen. See how Vietnamese says *answer* as "pay word give"? This is just like Fon and Haitian Creole, where *bring* is "take-give." This is one of many ways in which Vietnamese structure is, oddly enough, highly similar to that of many West African languages and, by extension, Caribbean creoles. For one, like West African languages, Vietnamese uses tones, and also notice that the Vietnamese say "person that" instead of "that person" just like Fon has "person the." A person from Togo or Benin would find themselves rather at home in Vietnamese just as we do learning Spanish or German, even though there is no relationship between African languages and Vietnamese. This is also true of the Hmong language that many immigrants from Laos speak.

Tagalog

There are about seventy languages spoken in the Philippines, but the one used as a common language throughout the islands is Tagalog (tuh-GAH-lug), also known as Filipino. Tagalog is related not to Asian languages like Chinese, Japanese, and Korean, but to Indonesian, and more distantly, the languages of South Sea islands like Fiji, Samoa, and Tahiti.

Tagalog speakers treat their verbs the way jazz musicians treat a song. To express even basic concepts, one must decorate basic verbs with riffs, fills, lead-ins, and tags worthy of Charlie Parker. For one, while we English speakers are used to adding a concept to a word by tacking something to the end *walked*) or at the beginning *re-read*), Tagalog can also insert something into the middle of a word. The word for "write," for instance, is *sulat*. To make an infinitive and say "to write," you shove *-um-* into the middle of *sulat* to create *sumulat*. "Go" is *punta*, "to go" is *pumunta*.

If English speakers say the first syllable of a word twice—*ji-jiggle the handle*—they are either frightened cartoon characters or rappers in the 80s. But in Tagalog, doing this is nothing less than the future tense: *sulat* "read," *susulat* "will read," *punta* "go," *pupunta* "will go." You can even combine the inserting *with* the repetition, in which case you get the present tense (go figure!): *sumusulat* is "reads," *pumupunta* is "goes."

Tagalog stacks these additions up in ways that almost sound like the old "banana-nana" game played with names ("Chuck, chuck, mo-muck, banana-nana..."). "Build" is *gawa*. If you have something built, you don't use the verb "have," but add a prefix *magpa-*, so that you get **magpa**gawa. But then if you want to say that you were finally able to have a house built, then you add another prefix *maka-*. But the result is not just **maka**magpagawa, because an aspect of Tagalog's personal kit of sound interactions accessorizes things a bit.

Just as we turn *f* into a *v* before a plural *-s,* in situations like this it is required in Tagalog that you turn *magpa-*'s *m-* into a *p.* Thus, just as we do not say *halfs* but *halves,* Tagalog has not *makamagpagawa* but *makapagpagawa.* This is just "to be able to have built," though. To use this in a typical sentence where you referred to having actually *been* able to have something built, instead of the abstract idea of "to be able to have built," you would change that first *m* to an *n:*

> Nakapagpagawa   ako ng bahay.
> managed-to-have-built I   a   house
>
> "I managed to have a house built."

Nakapagpagawa all from little *gawa:* as you can see, if Tagalog were a musician, it would be John Coltrane and *gawa* would be "My Favorite Things."

And wouldn't you know that one Tagalog-speaking Filipino-American once casually told me that Tagalog had always felt pretty simple to her!

Tagalog is also a good example of the results of contact between different languages. The Spanish colonized the Philippines for centuries and left a great deal of their vocabulary in Tagalog. For example, take this sentence:

> Bumili ang bata ng tinapay sa   tindahan para sa nanay niya.
> bought the child bread   from store   for to mother his
>
> "The child bought bread from the store for his mother."

The *-han* of *tindahan* is an ending meaning roughly "at," and the word itself is just *tinda.* This is from the Spanish word for "store" *tienda. Para* for "for" is also from Spanish.

Since the United States' takeover of the Philippines in 1898, English has had a dominant influence in the country (which is why most Filipinos who come to the United States speak English well). As we would predict, English-speaking Filipinos code-switch fluently between English and Tagalog just as Latinos do between English and Spanish. Sentences like this are typical:

> **Ang laki ng** table directly proportional **sa ranggo.**
> the size the   to rank
>
> "The size of a table is directly proportional to rank."

Other languages of the Philippines that Filipino-Americans sometimes speak include close relatives to Tagalog like Cebuano and Ilocano, which are similar to Tagalog in general layout in the same way as Spanish is similar to Italian.

Hebrew

Hebrew was essentially a dead language used mainly in Jewish religious ceremony and scholarship until the 1800s, when it was revived as a living language and became the official language of Israel, spoken as a first language by children for the first time in over 1500 years. This was the equivalent of attempting to make Latin a living language despite its only having existed as a written language for centuries, and yet it worked. Today Hebrew fulfills all functions of life in Israel.

The first interesting thing about Hebrew is its alphabet. It is written from right to left rather than left to right, but in addition, gives only hints as to what the vowel sounds are. Thus, to say "The army of the heavens stands by him" in the Roman alphabet would be:

Ts'va ha-shamayim omed alav.
army the-heavens stand by-him

In the Hebrew alphabet, this is, (read backwards, remember):

צְבָא תַשָׁמַיִם עמֶד עָלָיִן.

where, for example, the second word *ha-shamayim* "the heavens" comes out as just "hshmym"; it is left to the reader to know what the vowels are. There are some hints: the third symbol from the right, *a*, could only be pronounced "ah," or "ay," or "eh," not "ee," "oh," or "oo," for example. There are also vowel symbols used in Biblical texts and children's books that alleviate the need to decode:

צְבָא תַשָׁמַיִם עמֶד עָלָיִן.

In general, though, reading Hebrew means becoming accustomed to filling in about half of the sounds of the words by intuition.

The second fascinating thing about Hebrew is the way it expresses verb tenses. In English, when we want to change the tense of a verb, we usually add an ending (*walked*) or put a little word before (*will walk*). Hebrew uses some endings for purposes like these (and some prefixes too), but the most important way it changes tense is to change the vowels inside. *Hu kotev* means "he writes." "He wrote," however, is *hu katav*, where the vowels *o* and *e* change to two *a*'s but the consonants *k, t,* and *v* stay the same. We do this with some of our verbs, such as *rise* versus *rose*. However, for us, these verbs are irregular, whereas in Hebrew this is standard practice with all verbs. Hebrew also takes it much further than we do. "He will write" is *hu ekhtov*, where the present tense vowels *o* and *e* switch places (and the *k* changes to a related *kh* sound).

To say "correspond" (in writing), you change the *o* and *e* of the present tense *hu kotev* to *a* and *e,* and add a prefix *hit-* which means "to each other": **hitkatev.** Thus, what stays constant throughout all of these transformations is the three consonants *k-t-v,* rather as if a building were constantly being gutted with only the steel frame being left intact.

This even continues into the nouns relating to the concept of writing. The word "writing" is **ktav**; spelling is **ktiv.** A letter is a *mikhtav,* and the desk you write it at is a *mikhtava.* Thus *k-t-v* is a kind of disembodied essence of "writing" in Hebrew, with its specific meaning depending on what is hung inside and outside of it. This way of doing things is typical of the family that Hebrew belongs to, Semitic, which also includes Arabic and the Aramaic that Jesus Christ spoke.

Amharic

What do Ethiopians speak? We would naturally assume that they speak languages related to the ones spoken by other Africans, especially the Sudanese, Somalis, and Kenyans near their country. I have an old coloring book that describes how Christmas is celebrated in nineteen countries around the world, with each description given in the country's language. It was written in 1972, and so the writers acknowledge that Africa is part of "The World" by including Ethiopia. However, they describe Ethiopia's Christmas in Swahili, which is indeed spoken in many East African countries but is as foreign to Ethiopia as German is to Greece.

Oddly enough, the languages most Ethiopians speak are related not to any language of Sudan, Somalia, or Kenya but to the Arabic and Hebrew spoken across the Red Sea by Arabs and Israelis in the Middle East; in other words, the most widely spoken Ethiopian languages are Semitic languages. The official language of Ethiopia is Amharic, the language of government and education, and just about any Ethiopian one meets in the United States speaks it, often calling it "Ethiopian language" if we ask, assuming—rightly—that few Americans have heard of Amharic.

Few cultures would appear to be as different as the highly traditional, largely rural African culture of Ethiopia and the ultra-modern Western one of Israel, and yet the languages the people of these two nations speak are full of parallels. "Evening" is *laila* in Hebrew, *lelit* in Amharic; "house" is *bayit* in Hebrew, *bet* in Amharic. Often the words have drifted further apart but you can still see the relationship if you look hard, like second cousins: you can count to *khamesh* on one hand in Hebrew, to *ammǝst* (the last vowel being the sound of *a* in *about*) in Amharic.

Just as French and Italian trace ultimately back to Latin, Hebrew and Amharic are the products of change in different directions from one original Proto-Semitic language. As such, they are an eloquent demonstration of how language change can make two languages put the same original material to highly different uses, with both results being "languages" all the same—something we are seeing a less advanced stage of in the different uses of *to be* in standard versus Black English.

In Hebrew, to say "you are wearing it" you say:

Atah lovesh oto
you   wear   it

In Amharic, you say:

Tilebsewalleh
you-wear-it-you

How could *Atah lovesh oto* and *Tilebsewalleh* come from the same place?

Some people like to keep the different foods on their plate separate, some like to mix all of their food together in one grand mash, and others fall somewhere in between. Languages are similar. Some prefer to express each concept or piece of grammar with one word, like Chinese varieties. Others, like Ojibwe, cram almost as much into one word as we do into a sentence. Other languages fall somewhere in between, leaning towards one extreme or the other. Hebrew, like English, is somewhere in the middle leaning a bit towards Chinese, having some prefixes and suffixes but preferring not to scrunch too much into one word. Amharic, on the other hand, leans closer to the Ojibwe end, and thus manages "you are wearing it" in one word instead of three.

Now let's take a closer look. Tagalog surprised us in being able to stick pieces into the middle of a word as well as sticking them on the ends. Amharic is odd in a different way, having combination prefix-suffixes that "bookend" a word with their two parts. Thus "you" in Amharic is *ti----alleh*, with *ti* prefixed and *alleh* suffixed.

Yet this is not as far from Hebrew as it looks. Hebrew has a "you" prefix *ti-* too, but it only uses it in the future tense, whereas Amharic has made it more general. As for the *-alleh* suffix, Hebrew has a suffix *-kh* that means "you" when stuck onto a preposition: *shelekh* means "for you." Hebrew's *-kh* and Amharic's *-h* are descendants of the same ancestor (the *h* of *-alleh* is a soft "h" sound rather like a soft *kh*). In Hebrew this *-kh* is only used for women, but Amharic uses it for men—as we have seen, languages often put the same bit of ancestral material to different uses.

Then there is this piece -ew- slipped into the middle of the word Tagalog-style. In Amharic, what is written as *e* is actually pronounced more like the *a* in *about*, and therefore -ew- sounds pretty much like the way we say "Oh" in acknowledgment of receiving some neutral piece of new information. (A: *Actually, there aren't any more pencils anyway.* B: *Oh—then why don't we order some next week?*) Now note that "it" in Hebrew is *oto*: -ew- (pronounced "oh") and the -o of -oto are from the same ancestral piece of stuff.

Finally, though, strip away the two pieces of "you", and the -ew- and you get *lebs*. Remember that verbs in Hebrew are skeletons of buildings: properly speaking, *wear* in Hebrew is not *lovesh* but *l-v-sh*, just like *write* is *k-t-v*. As a Semitic language, Amharic has "skeleton verbs" like this too, and thus *lebs* is a fleshed-out version of the skeleton *l-b-s*. It's not a long way from *l-v-sh* to *l-b-s*: *v*'s become *b*'s in languages all over the world, as we can intuit from the way we are taught when learning (European) Spanish to pronounce *volver* "to return" as "bowl-BEAR." Similarly, it is obviously a quick step from *sh* to *s*.

So the official language of Ethiopia is one that began with the same original materials as Hebrew did, but has evolved along its own way in terms of sounds and structures into a language so different from Hebrew that what comes out *atah lovesh oto* in one comes out *tilebsewalleh* in another.

Eritrea was the topmost province of Ethiopia until gaining its independence in the 1990s. The Eritreans we meet usually speak Amharic, but also speak a related Semitic language called Tigrinya.

Hindi

The family that the Romance and Germanic languages belong to is called *Indo*-European because it stretches from Western Europe all the way across Iran into India. This means that the languages most Indians speak are related to French, German, Russian, and Greek, despite the profound differences in culture and even physical appearance between Indians and Europeans.

As Latin is the father of French and Spanish, the "father" language in India was Sanskrit, the ancient language of the sacred texts of the Hindu religion called the Vedas. Sanskrit has since developed into a number of separate languages about as closely related as the Romance languages are to each other, such as Bengali, Gujarati, Marathi, and Hindi. Hindi is used as a language of general communication in India alongside English and is therefore spoken by most Indians who emigrate to the United States. The Urdu that Pakistanis and some Indians speak is essentially the same language as Hindi; Urdu is spoken by Muslims and has more Arabic and Persian words than Hindi, which has taken most of its foreign words from Sanskrit, like English has taken so many from Latin.

Hindi and its relatives have a very different "feel" from their European relatives. For one thing, verbs come at the end of the sentence instead of the middle, and not just sometimes, as in German, but always. Speaking Hindi also requires paying close attention to whether or not something was intended, more reminiscent of languages like Ojibwe than of French or Russian.

Milna, for example, means "meet," but how you use it in a sentence differs sharply depending on whether you met the person by accident or went to meet them on purpose. If you deliberately went to meet Apu, then you say:

Mɛ̃ Apu se   mila tha.
I   Apu with meet did

"I met Apu."

But if you just ran into Apu by accident, then it is:

Muj-he Apu mila tha.
to-me Apu meet did

"I met Apu."

Here, for one thing, for some reason you don't meet "with Apu" as you do if it was deliberately, but you just meet "Apu." Most importantly, if it was by accident, then it isn't simply that "you" met Apu, but that meeting Apu was "to you"—in other words, it is like suggesting that the meeting came *to* you from outside rather than being created *by* you from within.

We saw how in Ojibwe you use a different verb for *break* depending on what got broken. In Hindi, you use a different verb for *break* depending on whether things were on purpose or not. If you broke someone's mirror by accident, you say:

Apka shisha mujh-se ṭuṭ   gəya.
your mirror with-me break went

"I broke your mirror (when I tripped)."

Kind of like "Your mirror 'went broken' on my account, that is, the mirror was broken not with the beak of a bird that flew into it, but 'with' me." But if you did it on purpose:

Apka shisha mɛ̃-ne toṛ   ḍala.
your mirror I   break pour

"I broke your mirror (because you made me angry)."

Here, you use a different verb for "break," for one thing. And you don't guiltily *emphasize* that it was on your account by saying "with me"—the little *ne* after the word for "I" is a neutral, default little add-on, used even if you just mention that you drank a glass of water. Also, you don't say that the mirror "went broken," which brings to mind George Bush's "mistakes were made." You say that it "poured broken," which, believe it or not, is Hindi's way of indicating that the breaking was quick and dirty (if you tell somebody to hurry and up and write their letter and be done with it already, then you tell them to "pour it written"!).

Finally, much of why Hindi sounds so distinctly un-European to our ears is because of the sounds that are indicated by dots under some consonants in the preceding examples. These dots indicate that the sound is produced with a slight curl backwards of the tongue, and the difference between, say, a "curled" *t* and a regular one makes as much of a difference in meaning as the difference between a *t* and a *g*. For example, *tota* is "parrot" but *ṭoṭa* is "lack"!

Korean

No one is really sure what group of languages Korean belongs to: some have tentatively connected it to the family that Tagalog, Indonesian, and the South Pacific languages make up, while others suppose that it and Japanese are distant relatives of Turkish all the way over on the other side of Asia.

One feature of Korean that is particularly interesting is that there are special endings one uses to show respect for the person you are talking to, and another set to show respect for the person you are talking about. Like Hindi, Korean puts the verb at the end. Thus to say "The teacher is going home" to a friend, one says:

> Sənsængnim i cip   e ka-nta.
> teacher   home to goes

But if you say this, for example, to your friend's mother, then you use a special ending to show respect to her:

> Sənsængnim i cip   e ka-**yo.**
> teacher   home to goes

And if you say this to the headmaster of the school, then you use a different ending to show outright prostration before a superior being:

> Sənsængnim i cip   e ka-**pnita.**
> teacher   home to goes

Then there is the issue of how much respect you feel for the teacher talked about. If you are telling a friend that the teacher is going home and wish to convey that the teacher is an esteemed person, then you slip *si* between the verb and its ending:

Sənsængnim i cip e ka-**si**-nta.
teacher   home to goes

But if you are telling Jesus Christ that this respected teacher is going home, then you use the prostration ending for Jesus but also slip *si* in before it to honor the teacher:

Sənsængnim i cip e ka-**si**-pnita.
teacher   home to goes

There are even some verbs that have completely different forms depending on how high-and-mighty the person you are talking about is. The word for "eat," if your next door neighbor is eating, is *məkta*, but if it is the president eating, then the word has to be *capwusita* (notice that "Oh, mighty" *si*). Japanese is also very sensitive to issues of respect like this, and one of the main signs that Japanese-American and Korean-American children have not learned their parents' language completely is not being comfortable with these special endings and substitute verbs (both of which there are more of in Japanese).

Korean is also a good language for seeing how our English way of thinking of how sounds relate to each other is just one arbitrary system out of many possible. The word for "soup" is written (in Korean alphabet) *kukmul*. However, it is pronouned "kungmul" because in Korean, *k* becomes *ng* before *m*. This is as if we wrote *Pac-Man* but said "Pangman." This does "make sense"— notice that *k* and *ng* are pronounced in the same place in the back of the mouth, so that it is actually a short step physically from *k* to *ng*. In the same way and for the same reasons of physical proximity, *t* becomes *n* before *m*, and *p* becomes *m*. As logical as we can see this is, it just isn't the way we do it in English. But to a Korean this feels as natural as it does for us to turn an *f* into a *v* before a plural -*s* ending (*halfs/halves*).

At the beginning of a word in Korean, *l* is simply dropped (except before a certain few sounds where it changes into something else). This is not a "slangy" feature that a child would be corrected by his aunt for, but something *required* even in standard speech. We are used to some English dialects letting *h* go at the beginning of a word (like Cockney British "on yer 'ead" for *on your head*)—well, why not *l*? For this reason, the Korean last name we pronounce *Lee* is pronounced "Ee" in Korean.

Space does not permit me to describe other languages we hear increasingly often in the United States like Khmer (Cambodian), Tongan, and Arabic, but these and all the others are full of similarly interesting ways ordinary people casually express themselves every day. No longer a place where a few close relatives of English like Spanish, Italian, and German hide in the bushes waiting to come out at night while English is asleep. Modern America is nothing less than a linguistic rain forest.

Exercises

1. To open up students' eyes to different languages, make a list on the blackboard of several English words, and have students give their translations in their native languages. For example:

	RUSSIAN	HEBREW	TAGALOG	VIETNAMESE
HOUSE	*dom*	*bayit*	*bahay*	*nhà*
WOMAN	*zhenshchina*	*eesha*	*babae*	*dàn-bà*
...	...	...	...	...

2. Have one student teach another one how to write this nursery rhyme in their home language, or have pairs teach each other how to write it in each other's home languages (it doesn't matter if the translations are perfect or not):

   One, two, tie my shoe,
   Three, four, open the door,
   Five, six, pick up sticks,
   Seven, eight, lay them straight,
   Nine, ten, a good fat hen.

3. Have each student survey their block, church, or apartment complex to see how many foreign languages are spoken, and get a translation in each language of the sentence *He sank in the mud up to his ankles.*

Further Reading

Bill Bryson has written two books that are lively yet informative trips through English, how it began, and where it has gone. The first is *The Mother Tongue: English and How It Got That Way* (New York: Morrow, 1990), and the second is on American English specifically, *Made in America: An Informal History of the English Language in the United States* (New York: Morrow, 1994). David Crystal's *The Cambridge Encyclopedia of the English Language* (Cambridge: Cambridge University Press, 1995), despite its title, is less an encyclopedia than a gift box, covering all and anything you might want to know about English through time and space, all festooned with beautiful illustrations and lots of excerpts from texts of all kinds.

If you can find it at a library, I also suggest the video set of the PBS television series *The Story of English,* which vividly conveys through live examples many of the English dialects I have discussed. There is also a fine companion book version of the series that has stayed in print, *The Story of English* by Robert McCrum, William Cran, and Robert MacNeil (New York: Viking, 1986). A certain John McWhorter wrote a book called *The Word on the Street: Fact and Fable About American English,* which is a more detailed but readable discussion of language change, dialects, and notions of "good English," with a special section on the Oakland "Ebonics" issue. I can't vouch for this one personally, but some people have said it was okay.

In this short treatment I have only been able to get across the very basics of why even the mundanest of speech is based on unexpectedly complex interactions of sound, sentence pattern, and intonation. Steven Pinker's bestseller *The Language Instinct* (New York: HarperPerennial, 1994) is a useful introduction to this aspect of language, demonstrating that much of our linguistic ability is hardwired into our brains.

For surveys of the variety among the world's languages, Anthony Burgess' book *A Mouthful of Air: Language, Languages . . . Especially English* (New York: Morrow, 1992) combines informativeness with irreverent wit in a way that the British seem to be particularly adept at. Back in the day, Mario Pei was one of the leading "public linguists," and I have always had a special fondness for his *The Story of Language*. Originally published in 1949 (Philadelphia: Lippincott) this has been out of print for a while. However, it covers so much territory with such concise, elegant writing that I recommend seeing if your library has a copy, which they often do; it is worth the effort.

Index